Essentially JAPANESE

COOKING & CUISINE

Essentially JAPANESE

COOKING & CUISINE

Hideo Dekura

NH
NEW
HOLLAND

First published in Australia in 2008 by
New Holland Publishers (Australia) Pty Ltd
Sydney • Auckland • London • Cape Town

1/66 Gibbes Street Chatswood NSW 2067 Australia
218 Lake Road Northcote Auckland New Zealand
86 Edgware Road London W2 2EA United Kingdom
80 McKenzie Street Cape Town 8001 South Africa

National Library of Australia Cataloguing-in-Publication entry

Author: Dekura, Hideo.
Title: Essentially Japanese : cooking and cuisine
               Hideo Dekura; photographer, Keiko Yoshida.

ISBN: 9781741105797 (hbk.)
Subjects: Cookery, Japanese.
               Japan–Civilization.
               Japan--Social life and customs.
               Japan--Description and travel.

Other Authors/Contributors:
               Yoshida, Keiko.

Dewey Number: 641.5952

10 9 8 7 6 5 4 3 2 1

Special thanks to:

Claudio's Quality Seafoods
Kikkoman Australia
Kirin Brewery Australia
JA Kyoto Chu
Japan Airlines International Co. Ltd.
Japan Food Corporation
Japan National Tourist Organization
Japan Railway Co.
Nikon Australia Co.
Sunbeam Australia
Sunrice Australia
Wheel & Barrow Homewares

Publisher: Fiona Schultz
Publishing Manager: Lliane Clarke
Senior Project Editor: Michael McGrath
Editor: Kay Proos
Proofreader: Carolyn Beaumont
Designer: Hayley Norman
Food Photography: Graeme Gillies
Travel Photography: Keiko Yoshida
Production Assistant: Liz Malcolm
Printer: C&C Offset Printing Co., Ltd (China)

Acknowledgements

I would like to thank all the people involved in completing this book. I asked many people about food and its cultural aspects while I was in Japan. They all recognise that we are in the cycle of globalisation. Tradition is not static—manners and customs change with time. They pointed out the importance of understanding and protecting the tradition and nature of Japan, but they also realised that they need new challenges—and they have already started.

In Kagoshima prefecture, Mr Kubo, the owner of Izakaya Mambō and Mrs Kayano from Makurazaki-council showed me around Makurazaki-city. We visited a bonito factory run by Mr Nishimura, Sata's *kago-buta* (black pig) farm, Satsuma-Shuzo (prestigious *shōch*t company), a fishery union and a dried mackerel factory run by Mr Samejima.

In Kumamoto, Mr Fukushima from Kawaguchi-fishery union took us to Ariake-bay to see the preparation of *nori*-seaweed and introduced Mr Yoshida, a retailer of Kumamoto-nori. In Fukuoka, Mr and Mrs Furuno invited me to a seminar on their organic farm and shared their enthusiasm for organic farming. In Kōyasan, Mr Ueki from Kōyasan tourist centre introduced me to Mr Hamada, an heir of 'Hamadaya'.

In Kyoto, my best friend Mr Michio, supports me and arranges meetings with interesting people in Nagaokaky, which is naturally beautiful and has lovely people, including Mrs Namikawa and Mr Kitagawa, owner of 'Mizuho' *wagashi* shop. In Osaka, my wife's old friend Masako-san gives us news from *shufu* (housewives) and provided photos of Sakura. Yoshiko-san and Kae-san share the *shufu*'s recipes with me. Mr Masaaki Izumikawa provided wonderful photos of Mount Fuji from Yamanashi.

In Chiba, my brother Yukio introduced me to Mr 'Tempura' Kanda, and Inbanuma-Eel farm. Kikkoman soy sauce company in Chiba gave me a tour of their factory and Mr Yano took us to an Italian restaurant with a special soy sauce menu. In Yokohama, we visited the Kirin Brewery and tasted chilled beer. Mr and Mrs Asami treated us to their beautiful green teas in Sayama.

In Seki, Gifu prefecture, Mr Ozeki the owner of Yamakyú prepared a special dinner using local ingredients, including *ayu* (sweet fish) from the Nagara-gawa. His friend, Mr Kato is a master blacksmith for samurai swords—25th master Yorifusa Fujiwara. In Takayama-city, I visited Gifu-livestock farm research centre to see Hidagyú. In Shirakawagō, Mrs Kimura shared her story about her life.

Mrs Kurihara from Shizuoka-*wasabi* union introduced Mr Iida who showed me his wasabi farm. I really appreciated Mr Iida giving me the opportunity to harvest *wasabi*.

In Yamagata, a group of Akatonbo showed me how the younger generation is being empowered by supporting local agricultural industry and helping the environment.

In Otaru, Mr Nakamura, an heir of 'Masa-zushi', explained the importance of being a *Sushi*-master and stressed that saving the environment for fisheries is a key element to keeping the quality of *sushi*. In Niseko, I met lovely people who love their town.

I would like to thank my helpful friends in Sydney, Mrs Jill Eilaias, Mr and Mrs Takita and Mrs Carol McDonald. To my wife Keiko who travelled with me to take wonderful photos and to my little baby Yuzuka, who has prosperity in the future. To my son, Gotarō, I hope he can share the passion of food with us.

Lastly, thanks to the New Holland team, who have patiently waited and listened to my requests.

Author's Note

As a Japanese chef who has lived outside of Japan for more than two decades and who teaches Japanese cooking, I have noticed that my non-Japanese students are just as interested in the background and history of the food as they are in learning how to make *sushi*. I assume that this is because just teaching the technique is nothing but an imitation of style— but with some cultural information and some knowledge of Japanese cuisine as a whole they become passionate about the cuisine and better appreciate the Japanese daily way of life.

So, this book introduces the main facets of Japanese cuisine, such as regional cuisine and special ingredients and also acknowledges the people who have devoted themselves to keeping traditional Japanese cuisine alive.

Contents

Travelling and Eating in Japan

There are many different ways to travel in Japan. You may choose to follow the traditional routes or take on the challenge of modern Japan; it all depends on your purpose, your budget and your schedule. When I travel, I note where local people gather and what seems to be popular with them. This helps me find interesting places to see and things to do.

This is not so easy if you don't speak Japanese. Before setting off, do as much research as possible on the Internet, in books and magazines, especially if you don't have local contacts. It can be hard to find information in local areas in English, but you will find general information at Tourist Information Centres and large hotels in big cities such as Tokyo, Osaka and Kyoto.

Japan has all the usual modes of transport: domestic flights, rail, bus, rent-a-car and ferry. Although domestic flights seem the obvious choice for long distances, you need to consider the distance to and from airports and waiting times against the speed, frequency and convenience of the renowned Shinkansen bullet trains. The islands of Hokkaido in the north and Kyushu in the south are linked to the mainland by tunnels. Shikoku in the east is linked by a bridge, so most of Japan is covered by shinkansen, which can be economical for overseas travellers who pre-purchase one, two or three-week rail passes before leaving home. The pass lets you take any shinkansen, JR train, bus or ferry anywhere in Japan, interrupting your trip as often as you wish to explore at your leisure. Except for the Narita-bound trains, you need not reserve a seat except in high season. At larger stations you can enjoy an *ekiben* convenience meal, but I prefer to wait until I'm on the train and have a lunch-box meal from the mobile trolleys that pass through the carriages and offer a tempting range of food. The best thing about train travel is being able to sit back, dine and enjoy the scenery without any of the hassles of traffic.

If you have time but a tight budget, an economical alternative is the bus, which may take longer but allows you to see more local scenery. Good food can be found at the amazing *michi-no-eki* road stations on the expressways. Many of these complexes have spectacular scenic views. they sell fruit, snacks, lunch-boxes or even restaurant meals if you have time. Buses are also a convenient way of seeing the highlights of the big cities, especially if you have limited time. It is a good idea to check details at the local Tourist Information Centres (often near the main station) as some of these buses are free.

Ferries are good for inter-island travel. Some overnight trips, such as Tokyo to Hakodate in Hokkaido, are available if you have time. Relax and enjoy hotel-style comfort in a unique setting. A simple ferry ride from the mainland to Miyajima on a cold winter's morning, when not many locals travel, can be a highlight of your trip as you approach the famous red *torii* (shrine gates), which appear to float on the water at high tide.

Renting a car may seem convenient, but Japan's cities and expressways have hefty toll charges and regular traffic jams, parking is never easy and is usually expensive. However, if you are heading out of town, it gives you freedom to explore the road less travelled and you can stop at road stations for sustenance and even regional road maps in English—if you're lucky, though never be fooled by English written on the outside. Open the map to make sure it is in English inside too! In Japan, cars drive on the left-hand side of the road and most direction signs are written in Roman script. You will need an international driving licence from your home country.

Travelling with heavy luggage can be a problem, but Japan has relatively cheap and efficient courier services. I've found that Takuhaibin, Kuroneko (easily identified by its black cat signboards) or Kangaroobin get my baggage to where it needs to be, including the airport, in plenty of time. This service is available from airports and convenience stores, but is even cheaper from the company depot. You can ask at the tourist information centre at airports or railway stations. Luggage services are available at post offices too, but may take longer.

Japanese business hotels are basic, with small rooms, but they provide breakfast and there are many to choose from—depending on your budget. I have never stayed in a capsule-hotel, where you sleep in a tiny space and share a bathroom. They tend to be very cheap but are at least centrally located.

A *ryōkan* is not cheap, but a good way to experience Japanese living. Each *ryōkan* has a theme, such as *onsen* (hot springs) or excellent meals. *Minshuku* are private houses—similar to B&Bs. You can also stay at a Buddist temple. I stayed in pilgrims' lodgings at Shōjōshinin temple in Koyasan, Wakayama prefecture one winter. It was comfortable with a heater in each room, but the corridors were so cold we could imagine the tough conditions of the old days.

The Charms of Life in Shirakawagõ

Shirakawagõ in Gifu prefecture is one of the most famous mountain villages in Japan. It is not a historic spot with a prestigious shrine or temple, however it has beautiful scenery and its traditional old houses meant the village was proudly registered on the World Heritage list in 1995. These *gassho-zukuri* houses, which were built in the 18th century when silk production flourished, were designed to protect against strong winds and heavy snow using Japanese pampas grass or a special local building material call sone. I am always amazed when I see the gables of these houses; the roofs have a substantial slope and create such a perfect picturesque scene. However, these villages have not always found it easy to preserve *gassho-zukuri* houses. When their main local industries had declined people had to leave the village to find work, and in the 1960s the village was partially flooded to build dams. Under these circumstances, they lost thirty per cent of the *gassho-zukuri* houses. Finally, the loss became big news throughout Japan and people began to protect them as an important part of their heritage. People's attitudes have gradually changed to appreciate the culture and value of village life. We should not choose economic benefit over our heritage. Shirakawagõ is now a big tourist destination and a prosperous village. However, I hope it will not become too commercialised and lose its beautiful traditional culture.

In Shirakawagõ, there are many *minshuku* (Japanese Bed and Breakfast) where you can experience the local foods and stay in rooms where the floor is covered with tatami mats. Rooms are divided by *fusuma* (sliding screens). I stayed at one called Furusato (meaning hometown or historic village), which is owned by the Kimura family. I was introduced to Mrs Minori Kimura, the 83-year-old mistress of Furusato who had been living in Shirakawagõ since she got married. Before dinner, Mrs Kimura greeted us in our room. She was a charming and precious person who knew all about the local history of the once prosperous forestry area and about the edible wild plants in the mountains. She had learnt how to preserve food, using these plants, from her ancestors. People then ate wild rabbit, pheasant, and even bear because this was the only way to get protein. People's lives were so isolated and harsh in the mountains, especially in the long winters with the intense cold and heavy snow falls that they had to work hard to survive.

The local people valued miso as a priceless form of protein in their diet; however, the water around the area is hard because it comes from the volcanic region of the North Japan Alps so they couldn't use it for miso-soup. Miso was eaten with cooked rice. One day, the village people were working in the forests and as usual they brought cooked rice with miso as their lunch. Then they had the idea that miso might be rather delicious warmed up with the edible

wild plants. They placed miso on the *hōba* (ficuslynata) leaf, grilled it over a fire and found it was really delicious. Nowadays, this dish is known as the most prestigious cuisine in this area and it is called 'Hōba miso'.

Mrs Kimura (right) explained how to preserve the *hōba* leaves (above). When autumn comes and the leaves are falling, people collect them and bring them home. They rinse them thoroughly and blanch them in salted water to sterilise them, then let them dry naturally. When it's time to use the leaves, they just need to soak them in water for a while. Mrs Kimura said, 'The relationship between nature and human beings is that we should get along with each other. We owe what we are to nature. Living in Shirakawagō is co-existing with nature. I would like to give hospitality to my guests by serving food that I used to have.'

Hospitality does not need to be fancy, but full of knowledge and the love of nature and living creatures.

朴葉味噌

Hōba Miso

Miso on the hōba leaf

1. Soak shiitake in water for 30 minutes. Drain and squeeze out the water, then slice.
2. Combine akamiso, light brown miso, oil and mirin. Add to spring onion and the shiitake.
3. Soak hōba leaves in lukewarm water for about 10 minutes.
4. Place leaves on a grill or frying pan.
5. Place miso mixture on top of the hōba and cook with desired optional ingredients over low heat.

This is very good with rice.

SERVES 4

4 dried shiitake mushrooms, rinsed

100g akamiso or hacchōmiso (dark-brown miso paste)

100g shinshú miso (light brown miso)

2 teaspoons vegetable oil

6 tablespoons mirin

2 spring onions, trimmed and chopped

4 hōba leaves (if you cannot find hōba leaves, use aluminium foil instead)

Optional Ingredients

Mushrooms, spring onions, thinly sliced beef, egg or fried bean curd.

Geography and Regional Cuisine

Japan is an island continent off the eastern coast of Asia. Climates vary from the tropical weather of Okinawa in the south to the short summers and long, icy winters of Hokkaido in the north. Both plant and animal life reflect these climactic variations, resulting in distinctive regional customs and food cultures.

Weather patterns are so distinctive that the media makes annual reference to the *sakura zensen*, the Spring Front, a virtual wave of cherry blossoms that sweeps through the country from the warmer southern districts to the colder regions in the north. Along the 6000-kilometre stretch of Japan, people follow the progression of the Spring Front on television and radio in anticipation of leaving the dreary winter weather behind and celebrating the joy of spring under the cherry blossoms—the one time of the year when they really party outdoors. Everywhere people plan outdoor banquets which are part and parcel of *hanami*, cherry-blossom time, a major event all over Japan between late March and early May, depending on the location. There is a saying that it is lucky if the blossoms of a cherry tree fall in your glass while celebrating *hanami*.

Japan—Hokkaido, Honshu, Shikoku and Kyushu, the Okinawa archipelago and the smaller islands—have a total area of 380,000 square kilometres, little more than Britain and Italy combined. The population is about 128 million, with Tokyo the most densely populated area.

Tokyo was called Edo from 1603—the time of the shogunate of Tokugawa Ieyasu—now called the Edojidai or Edo era. With the exception of Okinawa, Japan remained under the feudal control of the shogunate until 1868, when it was defeated with the assistance of French weapons and militia. Government was centralised in Tokyo, where the population had increased dramatically over the 200-year period. During the Meiji Era, people started moving from the countryside looking for work, swelling the population even more. This trend continues today.

Tokyo means 'the eastern capital', which refers to its position relative to the old capital of Kyoto, established in 794. The castle-city of Heiankyo, in the centre of Kyoto, served as the capital until the centre of power was transferred to Edo in the 17th Century.

The region surrounding Osaka, known as Kamigata, flourished as Japan's third cultural and economic centre. The three major cities, Tokyo, Kyoto and Osaka and their surrounding districts evolved distinct regional characteristics because of their varying historical influences, their particular geographical locations, development of their economies and transport systems, their culture and the people's sense of identity. In total, Japan became divided into nine separate regions with their own climate, local government, lifestyle, food cultures and dialects.

Japan has a variety of natural resources and distinctive regional foods. The inland areas are well served by rivers and the surrounding mountains and the coastal areas abound in seafood, giving rise to distinctive variations in ingredients and cooking methods.

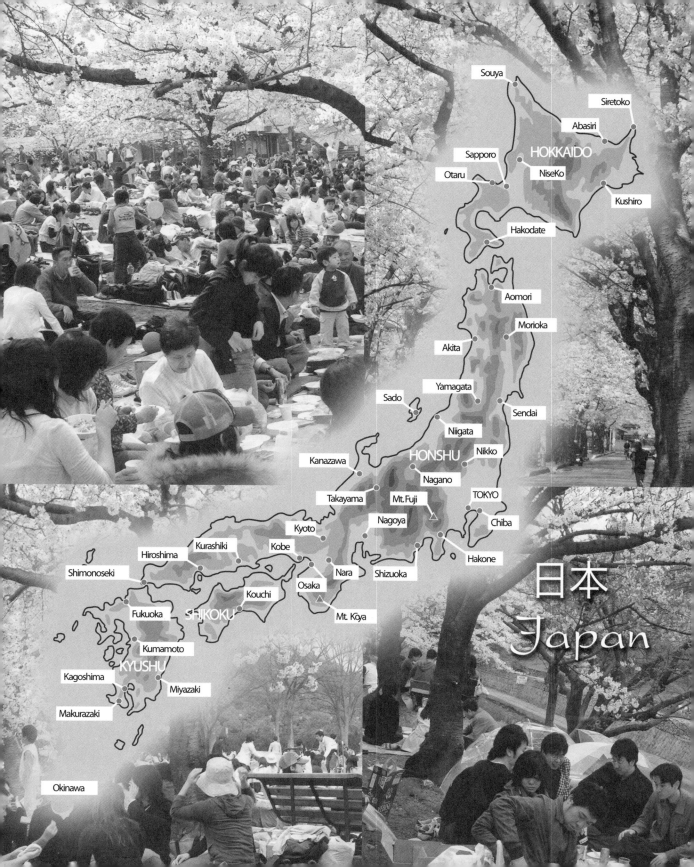

HOKKAIDO

Souya
Siretoko
Abasiri
Sapporo
NiseKo
Otaru
Kushiro
Hakodate

Aomori
Morioka
Akita
Yamagata
Sado
Sendai
Niigata
Nikko
HONSHU
Kanazawa
Nagano
Takayama
Mt.Fuji
TOKYO
Kyoto
Nagoya
Chiba
Kurashiki
Kobe
Hakone
Hiroshima
Nara
Shizuoka
Shimonoseki
Osaka
Fukuoka
SHIKOKU
Kouchi
Mt.Koya
Kumamoto
KYUSHU
Kagoshima
Miyazaki
Makurazaki

Okinawa

日本
Japan

Along the Japan Sea coastline and throughout Kyushu there has been considerable influence from nearby Asia and, even in the period of the National Isolation Policy, Western influence was rapidly adopted in Nagasaki, which was easily accessed by Western visitors. Western food was quickly adapted to suit the Japanese style in much the same way as new food is tried and reinvented even today. Tempura and kastera (Castella or Madeira cake) and Pan (bread) are examples of this custom and are still as popular as ever in Japan's current cuisine.

Japanese regional cuisine is inseparably linked to the seasonal celebrations and religious festivals of both Buddhism and Shintōism. The seasonal fluctuations herald changes in food and eating habits. For instance, *osechiryori*—boxes of prepared foods and nanakusa-gayu (seven-herb rice porridge) can be kept for three days over the New Year period. Throughout Japan the change of season is a significant factor triggering the desire to eat particular foods.

A new wave of food culture in Japan's more urbanised society reflects overseas influences as younger generations embrace an increasing desire for instant gratification. Country areas face a declining population as young people move to the cities and life is becoming more difficult for those left behind. However, there are moves towards highlighting the benefits of rural living, such as cheaper real estate, affordable living and tradititional values. This movement, known as *mura-okoshi* (village revival) is proving quite successful and is satisfying to see, as I feel the opposing forces of the new and the old must learn to co-exist in order to preserve traditional regional cuisine for future generations

Organic Food in Japan

Although Japan has long been identified with rice growing, we seldom think of it in terms of organic farming. This may soon change. In the heart of Fukuoka, a Mr Furuno runs a successful organic farm and I was fortunate to attend a seminar that he runs for farmers and others from all over Japan. Mr Furuno explains the principles of farming without agri-chemicals. There we were, standing in a field in the blazing summer sun, learning everything from how to prepare the soil to sowing the seeds to developing and expanding an organic vegetable business.

After the workshop they took us to Laputa, a successful organic restaurant in an isolated spot called Tagawa-gun. I was surprised to see so many people so far from the city. The key to their success is that—apart from being in a beautiful vineyard—they use only carefully selected fresh local ingredients and seasonings, are always developing new and creative menus and make their patrons feel at home. Their lunchtime buffet is particularly popular with an agreeable mixture of Eastern and Western dishes, not too heavy, and beautifully and colourfully presented. I was exhilarated by the whole experience—from the sowing of the seeds to the eating of the produce. I wonder what impact Mr Furuno's farming techniques and his training of so many farmers will have on the food industry throughout Japan.

Kimottama-Kaasan
Courageous Mother

In Japan, as in modern society everywhere, the rise of the nuclear family and disturbance of the traditional family structure has affected home cooking and the opportunity to continue traditional food culture. Everyone in Japan recognises the impact of globalisation. Traditions are not static, our manners and customs have changed with time and they are changing ever faster. This makes it very important to understand and protect the traditions and environment of Japan, but also be flexible enough to meet a new challenge. To reverse this, there are many grassroots activities occurring these days. Ms Etsuko Namikawa in Nagaoka-kyō, Kyoto, took action at a very early stage. She is known as a *Kimottama-kaasan* (courageous mother), who adores her home town, its local products and food. As a home cooking expert, Ms Namikawa regularly holds cooking classes and lectures about local life. She brings to classes for young people traditional Kyoto vegetables from her vegetable garden and talks about their goodness and character in season. Her Kansai accent has an affinity with the locals and her classes are always full of laughter. Ms Namikawa has also established a circle in which the members cherish special local products, and in using those ingredients they pro-actively participate in the movement to develop new recipes in Nagaoka-kyō.

胡瓜、チキン、お麸の胡麻和え

Kyuri, chikin, o-fu no goma-ae
Cucumber, Chicken and O-Fu in Sesame Vinaigrette

Kyoto is famous for its fu or wheat gluten. Fu comes in two forms, nama-fu which is raw and yaki-fu which is cooked. To make fu, flour and water are vigorously kneaded and the starch is washed out. Nama-fu is then coloured, shaped and flavoured using such ingredients as mugwort or green nori flakes and then steamed. Yaki-fu is leavened with baking powder and baked.

1 Trim the ends off the cucumber and slice thinly. Soak cucumber in the tate-jio (about a cup of water with a pinch of salt) for 10 minutes. Drain and squeeze out the excess water.
2 Squeeze the excess water out of the yaki-fu.
3 Sprinkle salt over chicken, then grill (broil). Once cooked, shred the chicken.
4 Using a mortar and pestle, grind the sesame seeds and add rice vinegar, sugar, dashi and soy sauce and mix to make the sesame dressing.
5 Sprinkle dressing over the chicken, yaki-fu and cucumber.

SERVES 4

2 Japanese or Lebanese cucumbers
12 small flower-shaped yaki-fu, soaked in water until soft
Salt, to taste
200g chicken breast tenderloin
1 tablespoon white sesame seeds, roasted
¼ cup (60ml/2fl oz) rice vinegar
1 ½ tablespoons caster sugar
1 ½ tablespoons bonito dashi stock
½ teaspoon light soy sauce

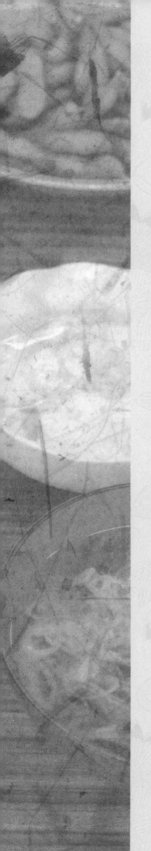

Niseko
A New Style of Home Cooking

Niseko is located on Hokkaido, the northernmost island of Japan. It has a total area of approximately 83,451 square kilometres and accounts for about 22 per cent of the total area of Japan but only about five per cent of the population. Originally inhabited by native Ainu, Hokkaido's modern development began in 1869 with the establishment of the Colonization Commission.

Recently Hokkaido has seen significant development and population growth with the capital, Sapporo now being the fifth largest city in Japan. Fisheries and agriculture have been the foundation of Hokkaido's growth.

Hokkaido has a relatively cool climate compared to the rest of Japan. Winters can be very cold with large amounts of snow falling. This is a great place for skiers, snow boarders and other winter sports lovers to consider as a holiday destination. Niseko is one of the best ski spots in Hokkaido and is famous around the world for its ski resorts and powder snow. It is called the 'St. Moritz of Asia'. Recently the number of tourists from overseas coming here in search of powder snow has been increasing.

Niseko is blessed with beautiful countryside and prosperous livestock and agricultural industries. Some Niseko women, who were later called Jyuugo-baa, (which means 15 grannies and middle-aged women), voluntarily got together and established the Niseko Process Foods Workshop, to actively promote the marketing of local products. They appealed to the community to appreciate the importance of developing local food and used their expertise to research and study local traditional food products and then to recreate them. They created a menu using mainly local products and ingredients, which they use in their daily lives with lots of love and care as if for the family; they are not genteel but they are authentic. When I shared a meal with them it brought back fond memories of good home cooking; it was food just like grandmother used to make.

Hokkaido and Niseko are not ancient like Kyoto, so the people there quite freely use modern ingredients such as lactic acid milk drink at their tables and are quite adventurous in their use of ingredients. Their dishes are not always strictly traditional but show respect to the ingredients, to nature and to people. This modernity has attracted newcomers from all over Japan who are attracted to the nature of Niseko.

Japanese Cuisine—A History

Japan's culture is a unique mixture of historic elements and a continuing stream of inputs from other countries both near and far, the foreign elements now arriving at an ever-increasing pace. This is only too evident when we start to look at what is happening in the rice industry. Japan's level of rice consumption has dropped considerably because there are now so many food choices, creating problems for rice producers. For a long time, the rice industry has been protected by the government and the lower level of consumption has led to the stockpiling of rice.

A national system of rice production was developed as long ago as 200 BC, which involved payments of rice as a form of taxation. From that point in time, Japanese food culture was influenced by politics and in some ways has been ever since.

In the Nara Era, (701–794), the ruling establishment operated along strong Buddhist lines, with strict laws forbidding the consumption of meat and strong condiments such as garlic, chilli and ginger. Subsequently, under the direction of the Imperial Court, vegetable cultivation along Chinese lines was established. The temple cuisine which evolved at that time was very simple, but by the end of the Muromachi Era (1336–1573) a more sophisticated style known as Shojin Ryori had been developed. This involved much more attention to the ways in which the vegetables were prepared, cooked and presented; maximum effort with minimum ingredients. More specialised forms of banquet-style cuisine known as Honzen Ryōri evolved for the court nobility (*kuge*) and samurai (*bushi*). Up till the Muromachi period, a system of *shokureihō* (food etiquette) had evolved which demanded high standards of correct placement and usage of particular bowls and chopsticks for specific foods. This became most evident during the meal preceding the *Kaiseki* (tea ceremony), which required a very delicate, controlled style of dining. Within high society, banquets were common and rather than being a convivial means of expressing their loyalty to the gods and their masters, they became more of a political power game of one-upmanship, a public pronouncement of allegiances. These banquets started with a greeting of sake, followed by a fine meal, followed by a sake banquet with entertainment such as singing, dancing and geisha. Whereas the taste of food had originally driven the evolvement of Honzen Ryōri, as it reached a peak, the visual effect of the food started to dominate, such that appearance and presentation rather than the taste or amount of food were the driving factors in change. Morsels of food, exquisitely carved, twisted, shaped and carefully placed on beautiful dishes were the order of the day. By the Edo Era (1603–1867), however, much of Honzen Ryōri had become simplified and the elegant banquet style was reserved for special events such as weddings.

In earlier times, depending on the time of day, *chanoyu*, the tea ceremony was performed. It may have been preceded by a formal meal known as *chakaiseki*. It was not until some time in the Momoyama Era (1567–1600) that Riykú, acknowledged in Japan as the founder of the tea ceremony, raised it to the level of an art form. The resulting *chakaiseki* is ritualistic and is more an expression of life's blessings than a full-on feast, it is a time to reflect, even meditate, a time to acknowledge the seasons and the design of the bowls, the plates and the presentation of the food. It also serves to ease the pangs of hunger before partaking of green tea.

During the Edo Era, the elevation of the status of merchant classes from their lowly beginnings to a level of considerable significance changed the balance of society, so that a broader range of food was accessible to a greater number of people. Formal dining and banqueting, which had previously been the domain of nobility and the upper classes, became mainstream Japanese cuisine and adapted accordingly. Further adaptations swept through the food industry with the opening up of trade in the Meiji Era (1867–1912) and again after World War II and continue to do so today. Despite this, among all the new, if we look carefully, we can still find the wonderful old traditions that have survived Japan's changing, well-notated eras. One of the joys of eating in Japan is discovering such a meal, imagining how it must have been in its heyday long ago and storing it up as a memory for the future. *Natsukashi*. (Oh, the good old days.)

25

Houchõ
Japanese Knife

The Japanese knife evolved from the samurai sword. It is single ground—only one side has a cutting edge—unlike Western knives, which have double-sided blades. Originally the Japanese knife was made from obsidian or quartz by striking, grinding and polishing. Eventually sword craftsmen developed a form of steel called *tamahagane*, which is only produced in western Japan in a high-heat smelter or *tatara* from iron dust and pure charcoal. *Tamahagane* is extremely expensive and difficult to forge. It was first used in the Nara Era to produce sharp, strong swords. It is the ultimate sword-making material and now used for knives as well.

In the Heian Era, cooking methods developed to suit the various new knives. In the Kamakura Era, *shōjin ryōri* (temple cuisine) spread advanced cooking methods around the nation along with knives quite similar to those we have today.

In the Meiji Era, Western knives were introduced. After World War II, new types of knives were introduced which, although still in the single blade Japanese style, were made from stainless steel which does not rust and so became very popular.

A Master of Swordsmithing in Seki, Shiga Prefecture

My friend in Seki city, Mr Ozeki, introduced me to Mr Katō, a man whose family have been swordsmiths in Seki since the Muromachi Era. He is a 25th generation master of *Kanefusa Fujiwara*.

During the civic wars in the capital of Kamakura, a group of swordsmith escaped from the disturbances to search for a new place with rich resources for sword making. They settled in Seki and invented their own refining methods. Gradually Seki became very famous for *tōshō* (swordsmiths) and swords. However, once the era of civic war was over, the need for swords declined and many swordsmiths started to use their skills to make domestic knives or tools.

Today, you need a special licence to keep a *katana* (samurai sword). *Katana* were not only used as weapons, they were also kept as a symbol of a *samurai*'s soul and fighting power. For the Imperial family or at the temple, a *katana* is a symbol of authority.

To make a *katana*, a *tōshu* needs secret skills, which involve using his whole body to judge materials and timing. At the workshop in Seki, I watched Master Fujiwara in action as he forged burning steel without hesitation and sparks flew up around him. It was such a strong experience I felt there was strong power residing in that workshop.

Restaurant Dining in Japan

If you want to dine out for *sake* and food, an *izakaya* is the place to go. *Izakaya* is often translated as Japanese pub, but is one of the unique styles of Japanese restaurants in which to enjoy *sake* (alcohol including *sake*, beer, *shōchú* and others) with food to match. *Izakaya-ryōri* (food at *izakaya*), is usually a small entrée or snack-size dishes. When ordering *sake* in *Izakaya* you also are served *tsukidashi*, a complementary dish like hors d'oeuvre. *Izakaya* originated in the Edo Era (1603–1867) as liquor shops that sold *sake* by volume. Later they started serving *sake* on the premises as well. Gradually they provided snacks to be served with the drink. Until the 1970s, *izakaya* had an image of a place for salaried men to drink *sake*, but these days the image has changed. They have changed the menu, furniture and interiors to attract women and family groups and to become more casual.

Aka-chochin (red lantern) is another word for *izakaya* because they traditionally hang a red lantern out the front as a sign. However, *Yakitori-ya,* where staff grill *yakitori* (skewered chicken) in front of customers—also serve *sake* and hang red lanterns. *Oden-ya* restaurants sell *oden*, a Japanese hotchpotch or stew made in a large pot. *Robata-yaki* restaurants have *robata*, a grilling fireplace and the *robata-yaki* chef uses a giant wooden ladle to serve the dishes from beside the fireplace.

Ryōtei are high-class Japanese restaurants, usually set in a *sukiya*-style building, which is based on a tea-ceremony arbour with a beautiful Japanese garden. They use ceramics by famous potters and fixtures such as hanging scrolls, paintings and furniture designed by leading artists, which are sometimes changed depending on the season, the occasion or guests. Using premium-quality ingredients, the chefs—who train for a minimum of ten years before they qualify—carefully start preparing some days before. *Ryōtei* provide orthodox Japanese entertainment, such as *geisha* and *gagaku*, traditional Japanese music.

Ryōtei provide the best environment to enjoy dining, service and food and are patronised by corporate executives, politicians or VIPs for confidential meetings. *Ryōtei* used to accept only regular customers with a reservation, not passing trade. However. since the Japanese bubble economy has burst, the number of meetings has declined and *ryōtei* have struggled. Their prices used to be so expensive that the majority of people could not afford them and, although some *ryōtei* still are, most now prepare a fixed-price menu to encourage visitors. Some modern Japanese restaurants now also use the prestigious name of *ryōtei* but serve meals in a more casual and vibrant setting—without the super-fine dining.

ジンギスカン

Jingisukan

Lamb in Hokkaido-style

In Jingisukan, a special dome-shaped hotplate—like a turtle's shell is used to prevent the oil and sauces from pooling and stewing the meat while it's grilling. Jingisukan can be cooked at home with a Jingisukan plate—bought from Asian shops—on a portable gas or electric hotplate at the dining table. This Jingisukan dish has a combination of vegetables and marinated lamb that is meant to be eaten as it is being cooked, so set the hotplate up at the dining table.

1 Marinate lamb in prepared sauce for at least half an hour. Heat the dome-shaped teppan and spread with lamb fat or oil. Place some bean sprouts with chives, onion, carrot and capsicum on the teppan. Grill for 2–3 minutes or until lightly cooked.

2 Place some lamb slices on the hotplate and cook for 2–3 minutes, turning once. Drizzle some sauce over the vegetables.

3 You can eat directly from the dome teppan, continuing to add more ingredients to the hotplate as required. Serve with Jingisukan sauce for dipping.

SERVES 4

dipping sauce (see page 182)
400g (14oz) lamb rump,
    thinly sliced
small cube of lamb fat,
    or vegetable oil
1 packet of bean sprouts,
    rinsed and drained
garlic chives, chopped,
    added to bean sprouts
1 brown onion, peeled and
    sliced in rings
1 carrot, peeled, sliced and
    precooked in microwave
1 green capsicum, de-seeded
    and cut into pieces
any other vegetable in season,
    such as cabbage, pumpkin,
    snow peas, etc

Seasonal Cuisine

Japan has four distinct seasons, each involving its own particular foods. The word *shun* refers to the time when any one food is in peak season and at its absolute best. At this time there is always an abundance of those foods and prices usually come down, so it is peak season for consumers in all respects. Japanese people love the changing seasons, always looking forward to the new products with the different cooking methods they bring. This can be quite a contrast to some Western countries where many foods are now available all year round and food seems to bear little relevance to the season. Symbolic of spring are *bonito* and *takenoko* (bamboo shoots), in summer it is *unagi* (eel) and (*suika*) watermelon, in autumn *kuri* (chestnuts), *matsutake* (mushrooms) and other varieties of mushrooms, while in winter *buri* (kingfish) and *hakusai* (Japanese cabbage) abound.

When new season food first comes on the market it is generally in short supply and the price is always high, if not extreme. There is a saying in Japan that each time you eat new season foods you extend your life by 75 days. If you believe that and can afford it, by all means indulge yourself. When a meal includes *nagori* (end of season vegetables), it is said to be enriched with the sentiment of a fond farewell for those particular ingredients, knowing it will be quite a while before they come around again.

Some events in Japan are also linked to the transition between seasons as they were once defined in China, but are now more notable for the symmetry of the days on which they fall, namely the third of the third, fifth of the fifth, seventh of the seventh and ninth of the ninth of each year. Collectively they are referred to as *sekku* and they relate to *Shintō* ideals of removing impurities, looking after people's health, happiness and safety. Each one has a connection with a particular food, a bit like pudding at Christmas or chocolate eggs at Easter, common for Westerners regardless of their commitment to the associated religious festival.

The first event of the year, *momo-no-sekku* (the Doll's Festival or Feast of the Dolls) is celebrated by eating such bright and colourful delights as *hishi-mochi* (triangular rice cakes), *hina-arare* (fluffy pink rice) or *chirashi-zushi* (*sushi* rice with chopped vegetables or fish, not rolled) and drinking sweet *amazake* (non-alcoholic *sake*). Families of girls must share (or endure) the delights of having their house taken over by a grand display of *Hina-ningy* , a set of dolls that represent the Imperial lifestyle at this time.

I love *Tango-no-sekko* (Boys' Day) in May, not only for the *chimaki* (food wrapped decoratively in bamboo leaves) or the *kashiwa-mochi* (red-bean *mochi* wrapped in a Japanese oak leaf), but also for the magnificent strings of *koi* (carp) kites that decorate all of Japan for the festivities.

Tanabata (the Festival of the Stars) in the heat of July, represents a time when two lovers re-unite in the heavens and is a time when people write down their romantic wishes on colourful strips of paper and hang them on a bamboo branch outside the house. It is fast fading from general popularity in big cities, except in primary schools, but you may still come across these decorations in rural areas. Because it occurs in summer, the most commonly associated food are somen, (cold noodles), previously cold soba and before that rice cakes.

The ninth of September is the official date for *Kiku-matsuri* (chrysanthemum moon), but it is celebrated any time from September to the end of November, depending on the area, with beautiful displays of chrysanthemums of every colour and variety—a veritable feast for the eyes. Traditionally it was celebrated with a cup of *sake* with floating chrysanthemum petals. Today, the tradition is in decline and often just an excuse to get stuck into the *sake*, if one needs an excuse.

It seems that some festivals have lost popularity while others have gained it. Whether it relates to changing lifestyle, commercialism or something more subtle I do not know. However, I can confidently say that those festivals that are still widely celebrated have become ingrained in Japanese culture and the foods that are so closely linked to them create an interesting aspect of Japanese cuisine.

Spring

If you ask Japanese people for a symbol of spring they will say *sakura* (cherry blossom). We rejoice at the coming of spring and feel nostalgia and wonder at the short life of the *sakura*. People start to enjoy outdoor activities as *o-hanami* (cherry blossom season) begins and picnics are enjoyed under the cherry blossoms all over Japan.

The first days of spring herald the arrival of so many wonderful seasonal foods including *sansai* (mountain vegetables) growing wild along the roadside or riverbank. Gathering and cooking these vegetables at their peak in early spring with their bitterness, individual relish and distinct flavours is a wonderful pleasure of the season. These days some *sansai* are cultivated and you can buy them in the supermarket to use in *tempura* and salads. Once you have enjoyed *sansai* you will never forget the experience.

Bamboo shoots are another food heavily associated with spring. In March, bamboo shoots of the new harvest are at a premium, but only one month later it is *shun* (the middle of the season) and a large amount of bamboo shoots come on to the market so that prices drop and people can easily enjoy a huge variety of bamboo shoot dishes.

In the spring fields, the beautiful yellow rape flower spreads. Rape flower is a plant of the *brassica napus* family, which also includes cabbage, broccoli and *komatsuna* (mustard spinach). Rape flower is sometimes used to make edible oil and is also used as a salad dressing. Today in Japan, canola oil is made from cultivated rape flowers and edible *aburana* (rape leaves) are available at vegetable stands or supermarkets.

Spring Produce

Vegetables: Rape flower, bamboo shoots, *sansai*.
Fish: spring *bonito*, garfish.

たけのこの白合え

Takenoko no shiroae

Bamboo Shoot White Tofu Salad

1 To extract the liquid from the tofu, wrap in muslin cloth or thick kitchen paper, place in a bowl, put a weight on top and stand for about 20 minutes in the refrigerator.

2 Julienne carrot, takenoko and konnyaku. Blanch in salted water and drain.

3 Combine dashi, soy sauce and mirin in a pan and bring to the boil. Remove from the heat, add vegetables and nanohana (or optional ingredients as listed on right) and leave to soak for about 20 minutes.

4 In a bowl, mash tofu with a potato masher. Stir in sugar, remaining ½ tablespoon of soy sauce, and salt. Add sesame seeds and mix through.

5 Strain vegetables and combine them with the tofu and any additional optional ingredients.

SERVES 4

300g momen-dofu (hard-tofu)

100g kintoki carrots, peeled (see note)

300g (9½oz) takenoko (pre-cooked bamboo shoot) —see note

100g konnyaku potato

4 tablespoons dashi (see page 78)

½ tablespoons light-colour soy sauce

1 tablespoon mirin

4 stems nanohana (rape leaves) or asparagus, trimmed

2 tablespoons caster sugar

Salt, to taste

1 tablespoon roasted sesame seeds, ground

Optional Ingredients

Beans, spinach (silverbeet), mushrooms, usu-age (fried thick sliced tofu), kaki (persimmon) and pears.

Notes

Takenoko are available from Japanese grocery stores. If you are lucky enough to get fresh ones, remove husks, trim and cook for about 30 minutes with rice bran.

Traditional Japanese carrots are bitter and reddish, but in this dish it is best to use kintoki-carrot, which has a sweet flavour after cooking.

Summer

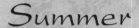

Everyone gives a sigh of relief when the hot summer arrives after suffering the inconvenience of *tsuyu*, the rainy season in late May and early June, even though summer can be rather damp and sticky too. In fact, it is often so humid in the middle of summer that, even when you are standing still, sweat oozes from every pore and you are likely to spend many a restless night unless you have air conditioning, which fortunately many people do.

I remember enduring the discomfort of summer heat in the days before air conditioning and the sound of mother hosing the front entrance in preparation for guests, and the deep, deep blue of the noren (traditional fabric dividers) hanging across the doorways inside, which gave us a feeling of coolness.

Even now, the spectacle of an ice-carving display of giant proportions in a fashionable alleyway in Odawara in the height of summer can have the same effect, but we also rely on the cooling effects of some of the foods we eat in summer. For instance, a pile of freshly grated *daikon* (white radish) on a plate suggests the iciness of a pile of soft snow and its piquant flavour refreshes as well as stimulating digestion. Sometimes a serving dish carved from a block of ice produces a wonderful cooling impact.

When I travel around Japan in summer, I usually feel like eating plain, simple food like noodles or eel. I feel it gives me energy. The roasted, wheaty flavour of a cup of cold *mugi-cha* (herbal tea) is one of the best, most refreshing summer drinks, though an icy cold Japanese beer is pretty good too.

Summer Produce

Vegetables: Eggplants, *Eda-mame* (green soy beans), bitter melon.
Fish: Jewfish, Spanish mackerel.

茄子の揚げおろし煮

Nasu no age oroshi ni
Fried Eggplant with Daikon

In Japan, several kinds of eggplants are used but the large eggplants common in Western countries are rarely seen. Ours are small and thin with a soft skin and delicate flavour. Eggplant can be stewed, pickled or deep-fried depending on the type. Round ones have firm texture with sweet flavour, they are good for stewing or dengaku (light deep-frying). Kyoto is very famous for its kaga-nasu.

1. Make 5 or 6 slits lengthways along the eggplants then soak in salted water.
2. Season okra with salt, then blanch. Drain and keep them under running water for a while to cool and keep the green colour. Slice diagonally.
3. Combine daikon and chilli and set aside.
4. In a pan, simmer dashi, soy sauce, mirin and sake. Meanwhile, drain the eggplants and wipe dry with kitchen paper. Deep fry in vegetable oil at medium heat or approximately 120°C (250°F). Drain well on kitchen paper.
5. Place eggplant and okra in sauce and continue to simmer for another 1–2 minutes. Serve garnished with the daikon and chilli.

SERVES 4

4 small kaga-nasu
  (eggplants/aubergines),
Salt
4 okra
4 tablespoons peeled and
  grated daikon radish
1 red chilli, chopped
200ml (6fl oz) dashi
  (see page 78)
50ml (2fl oz) soy sauce
25ml (1fl oz) mirin
25ml (1fl oz) sake
Vegetable oil for deep-frying

Autumn

In autumn, everything tastes better. The weather becomes mild after the scorching summer and it is the season for harvesting rice and many fruits and vegetables. Matsutaki mushrooms are at their most delicate in autumn. Matsutaki have an individual aroma that captivates people's appetites and although they are quite expensive, people are eager to taste them.

In autumn, nights are becoming cooler but the days are still warm from summer. Leaves are turning gold, orange, red and brown; it is the most colourful season in the year.

Autumn Produce

Vegetables and fruits: yuzu (Japanese citrus fruit), chestnuts, black beans, apples and grapes
Fish: samma (pike fish) saba (mackerel)

栗ご飯

Kuri-gohan

Chestnut Rice

Gardenia berries are a natural yellow colouring agent available from Asian groceries. They are used to colour chestnuts, pickled daikon-radish, noodles and snacks.

1 Crush gardenia berries and soak in water with chestnuts overnight.

2 Rinse rice and mochi-gome and place in a pan or rice cooker. Add water, salt and mirin.

3 Drain chestnuts, add to the rice and cook together.

4 When cooked, mix rice lightly with a rice paddle.

SERVES 4

3 pieces dried gardenia berries

20 chestnuts (preferably large ones), shelled (see note)

2 cups short grain rice

1 cup mochi-gome (short grain sticky rice)

3 cups water

Salt, pinch

1 tablespoon mirin

Note
To remove chestnut shells, roast over a high heat in a frying pan until the shell is scorched, then remove shell with a sharp knife.

Winter

Winter is the best season for hot-pot cooking.

In the Edo Era (1603–1867) when a basic food culture was established, a small table and a small hot-pot were provided to each person. The Meiji Era (1867-1912) introduced different varieties of hot-pot cooking, for example *gyu-nabe* (beef hot-pot), which used seasonal and local ingredients. The combination of ingredients in hot-pots are easliy adjusted depending on the seasoning available and the method of eating; in Tokyo-style *sukiyaki, warishita* (prepared *sukiyaki* sauce of stock, soy sauce, mirin and sugar), is used with beef and vegetables. In the Osaka-style *sukiyaki*, the beef is put in the hot-pot first, sugar is added and fried then soy sauce and seasonings are added. There are also other popular hot-pot dishes called *mizutaki, shabu-shabu, yu-dofu* (warmed tofu) *oden, yose-nabe* and *chanko-nabe*. I describe them below.

Mitzutaki

In Fukuoka, the local *mizutaki* is made by boiling chicken or winter kingfish in hot water and eating it straight from the pot with a dipping sauce—either *ponzu*, (Japanese citrus vinaigrette) or *yuzu-kosho* (Japanese citrus and pepper condiment). The idea is to taste true *umami* (deliciousness)— the Japanese fifth flavour in addition to the sweet, salty, sour and bitter flavours recognised in the West. Also added to the *mizutaki* are Japanese cabbage, spring onion, some mushrooms, *shirataki* (noodles made of *konjac*, a yam-like vegetable) and edible chrysanthemums. Sometimes *udon* (plain flour noodles), pork and beef are used. Finally, some people use the leftover stock, add rice, raw egg and soy sauce and make *zōsui* using the stock of *mizudaki* or just add rice to make a hotchpotch, medley soup. It's very tasty.

Shabu-shabu

To make *shabu-shabu* bring water to the boil in a hot-pot, blanch thin slices of beef a few times in the water, then dip into sesame and *ponzu* (citrus) mixture. You can cook vegetables, tofu and *kuzukiri* (kuzu noodles) in the hot-pot as well. Mainly we use beef for *shabu-shabu* but as another option you could use pork, chicken, *fugu* (puffer fish) octopus, snapper or pacific or snow crab.

Yu-dōfu

Yu-dōfu is simple tofu hot-pot cooking. The dipping sauce is a mixture of soy sauce, sake, mirin and stock or *ponzu*. The condiment is spring onions, *yuzu* (Japanese citrus), *daikon-oroshi* (grated white radish) and shaved bonito flakes.

Oden

Oden is made with a stock of bonito flakes and kelp. Soy sauce is added later. Then *konnyaku*, *daikon*, boiled egg and other various ingredients are cooked in the stock. Depending on family choice some people use many different ingredients. By the way, in Osaka *oden* is called *kantou-daki*.

Yose-nabe

Yose-nabe uses a variety of vegetables, fish and shellfish (crustaceans). This hot-pot usually uses bonito stock, kelp, mushrooms and shellfish. The seasoning is salt, soy sauce, sake and miso. White miso is generally used for *yose-nabe*. We also use grilled tofu, fried bean curd and fish cake but it can vary greatly. At the end of the cooking, noodles or rice are added to the pot and finally it's all eaten together.

Chanko-nabe

Chanko-nabe is a high calorie power food, which Sumo wrestlers eat. *Motsu-nabe* uses the organs of cows or pigs, which are cooked in a soy sauce or miso-flavoured stock. *Ishikari-nabe* mainly uses salmon. *Kimchee-nabe* is a very popular Korean-style *kimchee* (pickled chilli *haku-sai*) hot-pot in Japan.

Winter produce

Vegetables and fruits: turnip, *daikon*, *haku-sai* and *gobou* (burdock) and citrus fruits.
Fish: tilefish, kingfish and hokke.

水炊き

Mizutaki

Chicken Hot-Pot in Fukuoka Style

Mizutaki means chicken simmered on the bone in water without using any seasoning. This is a traditional method of cooking (mizu means water, and daki or taki means to cook). A donabe (earthenware pot) is an ideal pot for this dish. Instead of using chicken, you may also choose to use thinly sliced beef or pork.

1 To make chicken stock, put chicken bones in a large pot—cover with cold water. Bring to boil and skim off surface fat with a ladle. Simmer for 1-2 hours. Strain.

2 Wipe the sheet of kelp and soak in 1½ litres (2¼ pints) of water for 30 minutes.

3 Put chicken wings in an earthenware pot, pour over the kelp and the water it was soaked in. Bring it to the boil and add sake. Simmer with a lid on for half an hour, occasionally skimming off any surface fat.

4 Add chicken thigh and sufficient chicken stock to pot, cook for a further half an hour.

5 Leave to cool for 1 hour with a lid on.

6 To make dipping sauce, mix all ingredients.

7 Add vegetables and tofu to pot.

8 Serve the pot in the centre of table with a portable gas stove, if possible.

9 Eat chicken, tofu and vegetables with dipping sauce.

SERVES 4

Note
You can use the stock from Mizutaki to make zōni (Japanese soup with mochi rice cakes) or zosui (Japanese rice soup). To make zosui, add rice to the stock and cook. Finish with whisked egg and salt or light-coloured soy sauce for seasoning.

3 chicken carcasses, chopped into 3–4 pieces each
8 chicken wings
1 sheet kelp (5 cm (2ins) square
¼ cup (60ml/2fl oz) sake
500g (1lb) chicken thigh

Ponzu - Dipping sauce
⅓ cup (80ml/2½ fl oz) lime or grapefruit juice
100ml (3fl oz) rice vinegar
150ml (5fl oz) soy sauce
50ml (2fl oz) dashi stock
Shichimi (Japanese seven spices), to taste

½ cabbage, chopped
mushrooms to taste, such as enoki, shimeji or shiitake
4 spring onions
200g momen-dofu (hard tofu)

Optional Ingredients
French beans or Chinese broccoli

筑前煮

Chikuzen ni

Seasonal Vegetables and Chicken in Broth

1 Heat saucepan. Pour oil in a pan and stir fry chicken tulips until hot. Add dashi and cook for 10 minutes. Occasionally remove scum from the surface.

2 Using a kitchen scourer, scrub burdock to remove the surface skin and chop into pieces lengthwise.

3 Add burdock, carrot, satoimo and mushrooms into the dashi and simmer about 10 minutes covered with an otoshibuta lid (wooden lid that sits inside the pan on the top of the vegetable when simmering) or a piece of baking paper the size of the pan.

4 Lightly stir-fry konnyaku in a frying pan. Add a little dashi, then transfer back into the remaining vegetables and dashi mixture.

5 Add soy sauce, sake, mirin and sugar and cook over moderate heat for 10 minutes.

SERVES 4

8 chicken wings (see note)

1 tablespoon vegetable oil

1 litre (1¾ pints) dashi (see page 78)

100g (3oz) fresh or frozen burdock

1 medium carrot, peeled and cut in a zigzag along the length of the carrot

4 small satoimo (yam) potatoes, peeled

4 fresh or dried shiitake mushrooms

100g (3oz) konnyaku jelly, sliced (see note)

60ml soy sauce

2 tablespoons sake

2 tablespoons mirin

120g (4oz) caster sugar

Note
Chicken wings should have the flesh partially stripped from the bone and inverted to form a 'tulip' shape. Konnyaku jelly Is made from the starch of the konnyaku potato or 'devils tongue'.

'I believe there is food as long as there is life,
there is life as long as there is philosophy.'

'I believe that deep inside the
Japanese people there is just
such a connection between
religion and everyday life.'

Religion

When you ask a Japanese person what religion they are, they may seem a little puzzled at first, but most follow both Shintō and Buddhist beliefs. This answer may surprise the average Westerner, who is committed to either one or no religion. In short, Shintōism is linked to celebratory, happy occasions, while Buddhism is linked to sadder occasions, such as funerals, which gives rise to their dual commitment. The Japanese have long been very spiritual people, so it's not surprising that many of their food customs are influenced by religion. If you asked a Japanese person today, however, they may not know that many of the foods they eat have their origins in religious customs.

As rice became the staple diet of Japan, a connection between the gods and the effects of nature on people's lifestyles evolved. Heaven, sky, water, fire and earth became the elements that symbolise the connection between god and man. Ancient tradition demanded that whenever there was a rich harvest of crops or a good catch of fish, food would be cooked and presented at the Shintō shrine to express appreciation to the gods for their gifts. Cooking techniques, which were a significant part of these rituals, eventually filtered into people's everyday lives and became habits that continue into present times.

The period surrounding New Year is probably the busiest time for Japanese families, when they prepare for the gods to come into their lives in the coming year. All family members get together for a big house-cleaning session, cleaning away the past year's dirt, dust and grime—symbolising out with the old, in with the new. In the kitchen they prepare *osechi-ryori*, which is food for the first three days of the New Year. They focus on foods that will keep for at least those three days. Just about all preserving techniques are used, such as drying, preserving in vinegar or adding extra amounts of soy sauce, miso paste or salt.

There are a number of reasons for all this advance preparation. The gods are being invited into the house and it is important not to disturb them with a big clatter in the kitchen. This is particularly significant with respect to the God of Fire, who is the most vengeful god. From as far back as the Heian Period, we say that we must not use fire in the kitchen during the New Year period. Today it is slightly modified to say we shouldn't work in the kitchen. Actually, the real intent of the custom is to give women a much-needed break from the demands of the kitchen for three days.

In the middle of the 6th century, Buddhism was introduced through China and *Shojin-ryori* (temple cuisine) was also introduced. The word *Shojin* means a devotion to pursue a perfect state of mind, banishing worldly thoughts and striving for limitless perfection at each stage. The preparation itself is a part of the practice of Buddhism. An effect that flowed through from the Mahayana Sect of Buddhism into our eating customs, sprang from their ban on the killing of animals and the eating of fresh meat. *Shojin-ryori* is an extremely simple style of cooking with many restrictions. It includes only basic ingredients such as rice, beans and vegetables. The main principle is that meals are tediously prepared from scratch, using the most basic, original forms of ingredients, involving many processes and much time to get to the end product. Typically, soy beans are grown, harvested, dried, soaked, steamed, crushed, steamed again, shaped and left to stand in water to make tofu, before being used in such dishes as miso soup. Needless to say, the miso paste has undergone similar processes as well. *Shojin-ryori* consists of a variety of dishes but all are made in this arduous manner. Basic as they seem, the nutritional value is still there. They contain wholesome vegetables and tofu makes up for the lack of animal protein.

It has been through the need to produce food that would keep a long time that many of our everyday ingredients have been developed by people within and around the temples, either because they are in isolated areas or are isolated from mainstream society. Most temples play host to a considerable number of monks, novices and general workers who partake of two such meals per day. Where would we be without tofu, miso, *Shōyu* (soy sauce), *yuba* (bean curd sheets), *natto* (fermented bean curd), *abura-age* (deep-fried bean curd) and soy milk, all products of temple cuisine?

大根と油揚げの味噌汁

Daikon to abura-age no miso shiru

Daikon and Beancurd Miso Soup

1 Heat dashi in a pan and add daikon, carrot and abura-age. Cook for 10 minutes over moderate heat.
2 Combine miso and mirin, then add to the soup. Stir gently.
3 When it has come up to the boil, remove from the heat.
4 Pour soup into individual bowls and garnish with spring onion.
5 Sprinkle shichimi on top.

SERVES 4

800ml dashi (see page 78)
160g (5oz) daikon, peeled and julienned
100g (3oz) carrot, peeled and julienned
1 abura-age (deep-fried bean curd), sliced
80g (3oz) light brown miso
1 tablespoon mirin
1 stem spring onion, trimmed and sliced diagonally
Shichimi (Japanese seven spices) powder, to serve

Visiting Kôyasan (Mt Koya) and goma-dõfu (sesame tofu)

Kôyasan is a sacred place and an active monastic centre founded 12 centuries ago by the priest Kûkai (posthumously known as Kôbô Daishi) for the study and practice of Esoteric Buddhism. Mount Koya is 800 metres above sea level and since 2004 has been on the World Heritage List of the United Nations Educational, Scientific and Cultural Organization (UNESCO) as part of the 'Sacred Sites and Pilgrimage Routes in the Kii Mountain Range'. Kôyasan continues to attract visitors, including believers and devotees from around the world. It is an important destination for pilgrims returning from the 'Pilgrimage to the 88 Temples of Shikoku' and a sacred place that always welcomes people with Buddha's great love.

Many temples in Kôyasan offer lodging with *shojin-ryori* (temple cuisine). Based upon the *sôbô* (monks') nutritious vegetarian cooking, rooted in Buddhist mental training, this cuisine features simple refinements, a sense of the seasons and the five methods, five tastes and five colours. One ingredient that originated in Kôyasan is *kyõadõfu* (freeze-dried tofu). It is said that this was originally made with the aid of the bitter winter wind, which removed any moisture—you reconstitute it in water and it is used in stews and *maki-zushi*. A common dish is *goma-dôfu*, roasted white sesame seeds ground and boiled with *kudzu* (Japanese pea) starch. Its unique sticky taste comes from the grinding of the seeds. *Goma-dôfu* is served with *wasabi-soy* sauce as a meal or with white or black sugar syrup as dessert.

I found a *goma-dofu* shop in Kôyasan called Hamadaya that is over 100 years old. Sesame tofu uses *goma* and *kuzu* vines and also natural spring water from Kôyasan that is full of naturally occurring minerals. *Goma-dõfu is* pale white in colour and has a deeply delicious aromatic flavour that is hard to explain. It has a very delicate texture and melts in the mouth with a clear sharp taste and the flavour of sesame and mild *kuzu* vine. The secret to achieving this elegant flavour is the extensive kneading of raw sesame seeds. The correct technique is said to involve a minimum of ten years experience. Mr Hamada, the owner of Hamadaya, said that making *goma-dofu* made him appreciate Buddha's kindness and he actually recites Japanese Buddhist scriptures for the god of fire and water before he starts and during each step of the process. When I watched him making *goma-dõfu* I imagined seeing Buddha's figure. Such a wonderful masterpiece!

胡麻豆腐

Goma-dõfu
Sesame Tofu

To save time while making this dish, you can substitute sesame paste for the sesame seeds.

1 Wipe the kelp sheet and soak in 3½ cups (875ml/1½pts) water for 30 minutes. To make kelp-dashi, bring this to the boil and simmer for 3 minutes. Remove kelp from liquid.

2 Grind sesame seeds using a surikogi (a Japanese-style pestle and a mortar), slowly adding sake drop by drop until it reaches a creamy texture.

3 Add kelp-dashi to the sesame seeds and mix.

4 Strain mixture through a muslin cloth over a saucepan.

5 Add kuzu-powder and salt to liquid. Simmer for about 20–30 minutes or until it thickens.

6 Transfer into an 8-cup mould and shake gently to remove air bubbles.

7 Stand in a tray of water to cool. Cover with plastic wrap and refrigerate until firm.

8 Mix bonito-dashi and soy sauce. Serve with dashi and wasabi.

SERVES 8

1 x 5cm (2in) square kelp sheet

1 cup roasted sesame seeds
—you can also use black sesame seeds.

½ cup (125ml/4fl oz) sake

½ cup (125ml/4fl oz) kuzu powder (Japanese arrowroot potato)

1 teaspoon salt

1 cup (250ml/8fl oz) bonito-dashi

1 tablespoon soy sauce

Wasabi paste, to serve

豆腐

Tōfu

You will need a food processor, a thermometer, a piece of muslin cloth and a mould to make tofu. Use a cake mould or a milk carton. Choose a mould large enough to hold soy milk with some room to spare.

1 Soak soy beans in enough water to cover for about 8 hours in summer or about 12 hours in winter. Drain.

2 Using a food processor, blend soy beans and 4 cups of fresh water to a smooth creamy consistency. Transfer into a deep pot or saucepan.

3 Add another 6 cups of water to the pot and bring to the boil. Turn down the heat to low and cook for 15 minutes, stirring occasionally with a spatula.

4 Line a strainer with a muslin cloth and place over a large bowl. Strain soy beans. Wring soy milk out of the cloth using hands or a rolling pin. Do not burn yourself.

5 Now you have soy milk to make tofu in the bowl and okara (tofu lees) in the cloth.

8 Measure 400ml soy milk and heat in a pan over low heat until warm; 85°C (170°F). Remove from the heat and stir in nigari and combine well.

9 Pour into a mould through the muslin cloth. Place a bowl or tray underneath the mould and a wet cloth over the top. Top with a weight. Wait for about 20 minutes. To check the texture, carefully lift the weight off. If the pattern of the weight can be seen on the surface of the tofu, the texture is correct. If not, leave the weight on for few more minutes and check again. Take out tofu and soak it in water for about 30 minutes.

10 To serve, spoon into a bowl and garnish with green soy beans, grated ginger and soy sauce.

SERVES 4

300g (9½ oz) soy beans, rinsed, or 400ml sugar-free soy milk
10 cups water
30ml nigari (magnesium chloride) —see note
12 edamame (fresh or frozen green soy beans), cooked, to serve
4 tablespoons grated ginger
soy sauce, to serve

Note
Nigari is available from Japanese grocery shops. Follow the directions on the label.

卯の花

Unohana
Tofu Lees Salad

1 Cut off the stems of the shiitake mushrooms. Soak them in enough water to cover for about 15 minutes or until tender. Drain and reserve shiitake stock.

2 To prepare usu-age, bring water to the boil and blanch to remove unwanted oil. Drain then slice.

3 Combine caster sugar, soy sauce, mirin, 5 tablespoons of shiitake stock and sake in a saucepan. Cook for about 2 minutes over low heat. Add shiitake, usu-age, carrot, and hijiki and cook for another about 3 minutes. Add okara and combine well, then add snow peas.

SERVES 4

4 dried shiitake mushrooms, soaked in water

¼ usu-age (deep-fried sliced tofu)

⅓ cup caster sugar

⅓ cup (80ml/2½ fl oz) soy sauce

1 tablespoon mirin

1 tablespoon sake

½ carrot, peeled and cut into thin sticks

1 teaspoon hijiki (seaweed), soaked in water and drained

2 cups (500ml/16fl oz) okara (tofu lees—see note)

8 snow peas (mange tout/sugar peas), trimmed and sliced

Note
Okara is available from Japanese grocery shops.

がんもどき

Ganmodoki

Fried Tofu Cake with Vegetables

1 Break up tofu and leave in strainer for 30 minutes to drain off excess water.
2 Slice ki-kurage.
3 Blanch carrot, ki-kurage and snow peas.
4 Transfer tofu into a bowl and mix in yama-imo powder with your hands.
5 Add vegetables and combine well.
6 Divide into 8 and form into balls. Flatten the balls.
7 Heat the oil in a pan to around 180°C (350°F).
8 Deep fry tofu cakes until light brown, occasionally turning.
9 Drain well, and serve with soy sauce and grated ginger.

SERVES 4

500g (1lb) momen dōfu
  (firm tofu)
4 dried ki-kurage (black fungi),
  soaked in water
100g (3oz) carrot, peeled and
  sliced thinly
4 snow peas, hulled and sliced
  thinly
100g (3oz) yama-imo (Japanese
  mountain potato) powder
Vegetable oil, for deep frying
1 tablespoon soy sauce
1 teaspoon grated ginger

Note

Ganmodoki can also be served in a clear soup. They may also be cooked in a stock with mirin and soy sauce. Ganmodoki may be eaten hot or at room temperature.

   To test if the oil is hot enough for deep-frying, dip the end of a chopstick into the pan and if bubbles appear, the oil is ready.

とうふの味噌汁

Tõfu no miso shiru

Tofu Miso Soup

1 Mix miso and mirin together.
2 Slice tofu into small dice.
3 Warm up dashi and before it reaches boiling point add miso and tofu.
4 Reheat, but before it boils remove from the heat and serve in individual bowls.
5 Top with spring onion.

SERVES 4

120g (4oz) shinshú (light brown miso)
1 tablespoon mirin
200g (6½ oz) silken tofu
800ml (1⅓ pints) dashi (see page 78)
1 stem spring onion, chopped

Primary Japanese Ingredients

Dashi (stock/broth)

Dashi is the most fundamental flavour in Japanese cooking. It is made by boiling water with kelp, bonito flakes, mackerel flakes or dried anchovies, but can be made from dried mushrooms soaked in water. Add soy sauce, *mirin*, sake, sugar or miso into *dashi* to add flavour. It is used in soup, hot-pots and many other recipes. Today, instant *dashi* is popular either as a liquid or powder.

Shõyu (soy sauce)

Soy sauce is a most useful ingredient in cooking. It is a fermented sauce made from soy beans and wheat. It can be used as a versatile seasoning, in cooking or as a base for soup. There are five variations of soy sauce, depending on ingredients and character: *koikuchi* (standard soy sauce), *usukuchi* (light-coloured soy sauce), *tamari* (thickened soy sauce), *sai-shikomi* (repeatedly fermentated) and *shiro* (almost clear soy sauce). *Koikuchi* is popular, especially in the Kantou area, while the lighter but more salty *usukuchi* is preferred in the Kansai area, often used in soups and stews where it does not affect the natural colour of the other ingredients. *Tamari* has a rich flavour and is used in *sashimi*. *Sai-shikomi* originated in Kyushu. It has a rich flavour, colour and texture and is good for *sushi* and *sashimi*. *Shiro* is very salty with some sweetness. It has the shortest shelf life of the five. New health-conscious products such as low-salt soy sauce are now being introduced as are pre-mixes, such as *dashi* with soy sauce for noodles.

I visited 'soy sauce town' in Noda in Chiba prefecture, home of the world-famous Kikkoman factory. When I left the train at Noda station and stepped into the town, I could smell the aroma of soy sauce. In the Edo Era, Noda had a flourishing soy sauce industry using water transport along the Edowaga (Edo River) to the Edo (Tokyo) area. Kikkoman still makes a very special soy sauce in a small factory that is built in a traditional style and looks like a Japanese castle. This sauce called *goyogura* is especially for the Japanese Imperial household and is made from entirely Japanese ingredients using traditional methods of production. The factory also serves as a museum of soy sauce making.

Mirin (sweet cooking sake)

Mirin is a type of sweet *sake* used in cooking. It has 40–50 per cent sugar content, approximately 14 per cent alcohol and it is about a third as sweet as caster sugar. The raw materials are sticky rice, rice malt and *shōchú* (Japanese spirit). *Mirin* is used in stews, soups or dipping sauces.

Miso (soybean paste)

Miso is a soybean paste that traditionally played an important role as a source of protein that was rich in vitamins and minerals, but these days is generally used as a seasoning. It is made from fermenting soy beans with salt and the mould *kojikin*. There are many varieties that have different levels of saltiness, sweetness and colour depending on both the ingredients and the processes used.

Once *miso* was commonly made at home but that rarely happens today. When I visited the Minshuku Furusato Bed and Breakfast in Shirakawagu, the mistress, 83-year-old Mrs Kimura, made it at home. She said that in Shirakawa at the time of the civil war, defeated samurai enjoyed *miso* as a valuable source of nutrients. The technique has been handed from generation to generation. Mrs Kimura makes her *miso* in a large barrel every three years. She said she is too old to make *miso* now and she hopes there will be someone to take over from her.

Kome-zu (rice vinegar)

Rice vinegar is the main vinegar used in Japan, especially in *sushi* rice or in salads where it is used to make a vinaigrette dressing. *Ponzu* is a mixture of rice vinegar and the juice of citrus fruits (especially *yuzu* citrus). Add soy sauce into *ponzu* and it becomes *ponzu-shouyu*, which is good as a dipping sauce for hot dishes. *Sanbaizu*, made of vinegar, soy sauce and sugar makes a good dressing. Add *katsuo-dashi* (bonito stock) to make *tosazu*, a milder dressing.

Japanese Stocks

Japanese stocks can be made of bonito, shiitake mushrooms, kelp or small dried fish. They are hard to describe in terms of only sweetness, saltiness, sourness or hotness, you also need to include the taste called *umami* (deliciousness).

Katsuo-bushi (dried bonito)

Bonito stock is the most preferable *dashi* (stock) and is used in many Japanese dishes. In old days, bonito was just dried under the sun. Later, boiling was added and, during the Muromachi Era (1338–1573), the process was refined to the one currently in use.

First of all, the bonito is cut into more than three pieces, then cooked, deboned and formed into a boat-like shape. At this stage, it is called *namari-bushi*. The fish is smoked to remove any moisture, then coated with mould to cure. This process breaks down the fat, which adds extra flavour. At this stage, it is called *kare-bushi*. The process to make *katsuo-bushi* takes about four months—it takes that long to to gain flavour and *umami* and that's the difference between *katsuo-bushi* and *bonito-dashi*, which we can make in a short while.

Katsuo-bushi has a lot of *umami*—elements making it the essential natural seasoning for Japanese food.

Instead of bonito, sardine, mackerel, yellowtail and tuna can all be used in the same process.

Usually you can purchase already shaved bonito, but here are some points to look for if you have a chance to buy it unshaved. Good *katsuo-bushi* is covered with light grey-green mould. The surface is smooth; a rough texture means more fat. To check the dryness, hit lightly to hear a clear sound. Keep in an airtight bag and refrigerate.

Bonito-dashi

First *dashi* has a delicate flavour, good for soups, steamed dishes and dipping sauces. Second *dashi* has a stronger flavour than first *dashi*. It is more suitable for stewed dishes.

Bonito dashi—First dashi

Combine water and kelp in a pot and soak in for about
1 hour. Then bring it to the boil. Cook over low heat for
2 minutes. Take out kelp. Add bonito flakes and cook
over low heat for about 3 minutes. Then strain into
a bowl.

1 litre (1¾ pints) water
1 sheet kelp (approx. 10cm
   (4ins) square), wiped
40g (1½oz) bonito flakes

MAKES 1 LITRE (1¾ PINTS) DASHI STOCK

Second dashi

Use the bonito flakes of first dashi. Put used bonito
flakes back to the pot. Add the same amount of water
as before and bring it to the boil. Over low heat, cook to
concentrate until the liquid is reduced by half.
Add 20g (¾oz) of extra bonito flakes and slow-cook for
30 minutes then strain.

Note
It is better to use dashi on the same day; however, you can
keep it in a refrigerator for a couple of days, or frozen in a sealed
container or in plastic bags with a zipper. Bonito flakes can also
be used as a condiment for tofu or salad.

Rice Growing

Rice is Japan's principal food and rice farms are a key factor in the development of Japanese culture. The countryside is dotted with small rice fields and it always amazes me that rice is grown in such a variety of places. Land is at a premium in Japan and even in the semi-urban areas, tiny blocks are used to plant a rice crop. Being a mountainous country, Japan never suffers from a lack of water to grow rice. Larger scale farmers run their businesses efficiently, producing beautiful shortgrain varieties such as *Koshihikari, Akitakomachi* and *Sasanishiki*.

Until recently, rice growing was protected and subsidised. With increasing globalisation, Japanese farmers have to deal with cheaper *gaikoku-mai* (foreign rice), putting them under pressure. It seems their only solution is to expand their farms to increase productivity and profits. Visiting organic rice farms around Japan, I see another answer, which is to move towards organic production and create a market for organic rice, perhaps trading directly with the consumer.

In Fukuoka, Mr Furuno runs a successful, totally organic family business. In Yamagata, the *Akatombo* (Red Dragonfly) Farmers' Club—a cooperative—aims to maintain environmentally friendly farming practices and provide safe food to consumers. The Furuno family runs a model organic farm based on a system developed by Arata Seiko in Toyama in 1985. A hybrid *aigamo* duck eats insects and weed, while its droppings provide a nutritious fertiliser for the rice. While swimming, the ducks' feet churn up the mud, stimulating the growth of the rice. As well as producing excellent rice, Mr Furuno has the added bonus of selling organic duck meat. This well-researched method has proven to be very successful.

Red Dragonfly works somewhat differently in the cooler district of Yamagata. Concerned about the loss of workers to the cities, young farmers formed a cooperative based on three principles. Each farmer must be totally committed, use environmentally-friendly farming methods and be open minded about business—not limited to small-scale trading. They agreed to share machinery to reduce overheads and waste and introduced recycling methods such as using rice bran—which was previously dumped—for cattle feed. They developed a network between rural and metropolitan communities, tapping into a distributor of organic foods, known as *seikatsu-kyodokumi-ai*. Their produce has a reputation for being not only tasty, but safe and natural too. This approach has inspired local farmers to stay around and has inspired young people all over Japan to join in. It was satisfying to see the revival of traditional farming practices and ethics by this dynamic group of energetic and passionate young people. I hope it continues well into the future.

The Truth of the Grain
—The Lowdown on Rice

In Japan, as elsewhere, households are becoming smaller. Modern transport and easy access to shops has reduced the need to store large amounts of rice at home where space is limited. In country areas large amounts of rice that require longer storage are still likely to be purchased. Regardless of the amount of rice being stored, basic factors need to be considered.

High humidity and temperature increase the likelihood of mould growing or insects hatching in the rice, which is best stored in a cool, dark place—between 13°–16°C and less than 70 per cent humidity—not unlike wine-cellar conditions.

In Japan, rice is traditionally kept in large willow or metal containers called *kome-bitsu*. Today they are usually insulated stainless steel or plastic and store 10–20 kilograms of rice. Many dispense the required amount of rice at the push of a button.

To reduce the likelihood of insects in the rice, people keep a dried chilli in the lid of the container. With changing lifestyles, many people simply buy a 5 kilogram pack of rice and keep it in the vegetable section of the refrigerator.

There is no great mystery to cooking rice, but there is a certain ritual. Firstly, rice should be measured precisely and washed well, to remove the rice-bran coating on each grain. This should be done as quickly as possible because the flavour and smell of the bran will penetrate the grains as it soaks in when wet. To wash rice, put it in a bowl of cold water, stir vigorously with your hand, then drain. Do this three times, straining through a sieve when finished. Soak the washed rice in a bowl of fresh water for approximately 30 minutes and strain again. When rice is prepared professionally for *sushi*, it is soaked overnight in a cool room or refrigerator.

Rice can be cooked in a saucepan if you are desperate, but every Japanese household probably has a rice cooker. Place the strained rice in the rice-cooker pan, add an equal amount of cold water and leave for about 30 minutes. In Japan, professionals vary the amount of water depending on the age of the rice. Less water is required for fresh rice. Outside Japan, it is difficult to judge the age of the rice as usually it hasn't come straight from the rice paddy. Depending on whether you prefer hard or soft rice, the amount of water can be adjusted accordingly, with slightly more for softer rice. After you switch on the rice cooker, it will automatically start heating in about 20–25 minutes. Allow it to stand for a further 10–15 minutes before opening. It is important to stir the rice to allow the steam to escape and to fluff it up. Wet the ladle to prevent the rice from sticking and loosen the rice from the sides of the bowl, fold it up and over from the bottom with a quick but gentle slicing action to separate the grains.

Japanese typically serve rice in separate bowls, like other elements of the meal. Rice is eaten separately so its flavour can be fully appreciated, not swamped by other tastes. Rice bowls are not very large and are lifted from the table while eating. It is considered bad manners to eat rice directly from a bowl on the table. The rice cooker is set on a separate table or tray beside the mother, who dutifully serves up seconds.

Leftover rice is often eaten for breakfast or stored in an airtight container in the refrigerator for up to two days and used for fried rice. To keep it longer, it can be divided into individual portions in freezer bags, flattened, kept in the freezer and warmed in the microwave oven. Personally, I feel it loses some of its flavour and texture when you do this, but it is convenient.

Preparing Rice

The Japanese tend to be particular about rice—we think it is the deciding factor of the meal, but who decides what makes a delicious cooked rice? Everyone has his own idea of how to achieve the best taste and texture, depending on personal preferences, family or region. Here is a very basic introduction to cooking rice.

1 Rinse rice in a large amount of water, holding the bowl with one hand and stirring the rice briskly. Tip out the water. Repeat this action three times. Rinse the rice quickly otherwise it easily absorbs the smell of the rice bran.
2 Drain and keep the rice in the strainer for 30 minutes covered with a cloth.
3 Transfer into a rice cooker or a pot and add the same amount of water. Set the rice cooker for 15 minutes to an hour (more time makes a moister rice).
4 Switch on the rice cooker. Otherwise, with a lid on the pot, bring it to the boil, then reduce the heat to low and cook for 5 minutes. Over low heat, cook for another 5 minutes. Then steam for 5–10 minutes.
5 When the rice is cooked, turn it over gently with a moistened rice paddle to allow excess moisture to escape as steam.

4 cups short grain rice
4 cups (1 litre/1¾ pints) water—you may add more or less water for preferred texture.

やきめし

Yaki-meshi

Fried Rice

1 Warm rice briefly in a microwave oven. Cook peas and corn separately and drain well.
2 Break eggs into a bowl and stir.
3 Heat a pan over high heat, add a small amount of oil. Add eggs to the pan, stirring constantly to scramble. Transfer onto a plate.
4 Heat more oil in the pan, add garlic, carrot and spring onion and stir for 1 minute with wooden spoon.
5 Add peas, corn, and then warmed rice, stirring continuously. Add scrambled egg.
6 Sprinkle with salt and pepper and stir-fry for a minute.

SERVES 2

4 cups cooked leftover rice
½ cup fresh or frozen green peas, cooked and drained
½ cup fresh or frozen corn, cooked and drained
Vegetable oil
2 eggs
1 garlic clove, crushed
1 small carrot, peeled and chopped
1 spring onion, chopped
1 teaspoon salt
a pinch of pepper

Note
If you prefer a curry taste, add 1 tablespoon curry powder when you add the spring onion. For Tokyo-style fried rice, add soy sauce instead of salt. Other ingredients such as chopped ham, bacon, cooked chicken thigh or roasted duck may be added.

To make red rice, add 3 tablespoons of coloured rice (wild rice) when cooking.

焼きおにぎり

Yaki-Onigiri

Rice Balls with Miso

Onigiri is so convenient that it is hugely popular in Japan—in some ways it is the equivalent of the sandwich. We sometimes eat onigiri simply with salt, but onigiri can also be more funky. Traditionally, onigiri has ume-boshi (pickled plum) inside, but nowadays it can feature tuna mayonnaise or even croquette. Many varieties of onigiri can be found at speciality shops, supermarkets, the food corner at department stores or even at convenience stores.

1 Add a pinch of salt to a bowl of water.
2 Dip your hands into the salted water to prevent rice from sticking to you then place a spoonful of rice on one palm and cover with the other. With a little pressure, form the rice in to a ball.
3 With a teaspoon, spread miso dip over one side of the onigiri. Then lightly grill (broil). If you have a nori sheet, wrap it around the onigiri before grilling, but be careful not to burn it.

MAKES 4

Salt, pinch
4 cups of cooked short grain rice
1 tablespoon miso dip

すしめし
Sushi Rice

You will need a wooden sushi bowl, a rice paddle or a wooden spatula, a hand fan or Japanese paper fan and muslin cloth or kitchen towel to make sushi rice.

1   To make sushi vinaigrette, mix rice vinegar, sugar and salt.
2   Moisten the wooden bowl.
3   Using a damp rice paddle, transfer the cooked rice into the bowl.
4   Gradually pour sushi vinegar over the rice.
5   Mix the rice evenly around the bowl with a slicing action.
6   While mixing, cool the rice with a hand fan so that the rice absorbs the vinegar mixture and becomes glossy and the taste is enhanced.
7   Cover with a damp muslin cloth and cool it down to body temperature.

MAKES APPROXIMATELY 6 CUPS

½ cup (125ml/4fl oz) rice vinegar
⅓ cup caster sugar
1 teaspoon salt
6 cups cooked rice

Vegetables in Japan

Having grown up in Japan, it never ceases to amaze me each time I go back, how vastly different the range of fresh vegetables is compared to what was available up to the 1970s. I suppose it is the same in many countries, but thinking back to those times, we thought we were well off, because we had survived the shortages of the post-war period. Now, Japan really is well off in the vegetable department, as there is an abundance of fresh produce and we have the best of both worlds. In the past, we used to eat mainly vegetables that were native to Japan or those that had come in from the Asian continent. Such salad items as tomatoes or lettuce were rarities and we always ate cooked vegetables, never raw. Many were growing wild in the hills and were collectively known as san-sai (mountain vegetables).

Immediately after World War II there was a major food crisis in Japan and in order to overcome the vegetable shortage, high volume, mass production got under way. At the same time, we started to exchange ideas and cooking methods with other countries and newly introduced Western-style foods penetrated every prefecture of Japan. This resulted in some significant changes to the eating habits of the Japanese and a decrease in the consumption of traditional vegetables. For instance, until the 1950s, we used to eat a particular variety of carrots known as kintoki-ninjin or kyo-ninjin, which were a rather brownish colour and had a very strong flavour. They need to be cooked to be palatable; you could absolutely not eat them raw the way we can eat the carrots available today. In the same way that Westerners are surprised at Japanese people eating raw fish like *sashimi*, similarly the Japanese were very surprised at Westerners eating raw carrots. Kintoki-ninjin carrots are still on the market in limited supply today, but are only used for special occasions and New Year's cuisine.

Another such change is the common inclusion in obento boxes of some salad, be it coleslaw, potato salad or tomato and lettuce, which you would never have seen in a traditional lunch-box even thirty years ago. As I remember, instead of these salads, pickled vegetables were used as garnish.

These days, because we have more or less reached such a comfortable economic position in terms of our eating habits, we can afford to look back at what has been lost and are now starting to rethink traditional vegetables prepared to suit the modern lifestyle. There is a spotlight on particular vegetables produced in certain areas. For example, mizuna, which was always boiled, is now included in salads. This has been a big hit in Kyoto.

Apart from this, there have been some vegetables that have always maintained their position, such as takenoko (bamboo shoots). The last time I was in Kyoto, I visited Mr Yamada, a takenoko producer in Nagaoka-kyo, not far from the heart of the city. The Yamada family has an incredible history of twenty-seven generations of bamboo farmers. It seems they know everything there is to know about bamboo. Their bamboo forest is so well maintained and beautifully pruned that it looks like a prize show garden. When I stood in the soft light filtering through the canopy of the overhanging branches, some as high as fifty metres, I felt I had slipped into another world where no civilisation existed and I had stepped back in time.

However, I can see that in the real world, the Yamada family is very practical. They are conscientious people who realise that, even though their efforts are focussed on the once-a-year harvest in early spring, the forest requires constant, year-round attention. Because takenoko is one of the first vegetables to appear in spring, Japanese people take great delight in its arrival on the shop shelves and the dining tables, as it heralds the warmer weather and relief from the cold. Unlike many vegetables that are now starting to be available all year round due to imports, takenoko is considered particularly special as it is still limited to spring. Older people feel very nostalgic about takenoko, but for the younger generation I can see that there is already movement afoot to reinvent takenoko with new cooking methods. Mrs Namikawa in Kyoto is leading the way in this area.

Not only in Kyoto, but also in other areas, there is a slow revival of traditional Japanese vegetables. I was surprised to see nigauri (bitter melon) in Okinawa. As you may have guessed, this vegetable is very bitter and doesn't usually fit in too well with Japanese cooking. However, it is currently being promoted for its nutritional value, being high in Vitamin C, which they say is good for overcoming fatigue, which is particularily beneficial in a country with hot steamy summers. It is easy to grow and is now becoming popular all over Japan.

I expect that from now on we will see lots more vegetables coming on to the scene that will fit in with the new style of eating in Japan.

和風ラタトゥイユ

Wafú ratatoiyu

Japanese-style Ratatouille

1 Heat oil and stir-fry onion, carrot, burdock, eggplant and tomatoes.
2 Make kelp stock by soaking the sheet in 500ml (16fl oz) of water for 30 minutes, remove kelp.
3 Add bonito and kelp stocks to vegetables and simmer for 30 minutes.
4 Mix miso with sake and add into the soup. Cook for 5 minutes.
5 Add mushrooms and pi-man, and serve with parsley.

SERVES 4

Vegetable oil
1 medium brown onion, peeled and chopped
1 medium carrot, peeled and chopped
40g burdock, peeled and sliced
100–150g eggplant (aubergine), sliced and chopped
5 tomatoes, peeled or a can of whole tomatoes
5 x 5cm (2x2ins) kelp sheet, wiped
500ml (16fl oz) bonito dashi (see page 78)
2 tablespoons saikyo (white miso) paste
1 tablespoon sake
16 shimeji mushrooms
4 pi-man (Japanese green pepper or green capsicum), chopped
1 tablespoon parsley, chopped

もろキュウ

Morokyú

Cucumber with Miso Dip

1. Mix white and brown miso and sugar.
2. Heat vegetable oil in a pan over low heat.
3. Add garlic and stir. When soft, add the miso mixture and stir with a wooden spatula.
4. Add bonito flakes and mirin and mix again.
5. Stir through shiso and shichimi. Cool down to room temperature before using.
6. Cut cucumber into quarters lengthways and remove seeds. Cut into sticks.

MAKES 1 CUP (250ML/8FL OZ) MISO DIP

½ cup saikyo-miso (white miso)
½ cup shinshu miso (brown miso)
¼ cup caster sugar
2 tablespoons vegetable oil
2 garlic cloves, peeled and sliced
20g (1oz) bonito flakes
¼ cup (60ml/2fl oz) mirin
6 shiso (Japanese green basil) leaves, trimmed and sliced or chopped spring onion
½ teaspoon shichimi (Japanese seven spices) or red chilli, de-seeded and sliced
2 cucumbers

ブロッコリーの辛し和え

Burokkori no karashi ae
Dressed Broccoli with Mustard Miso

This is a side dish.

1 Mix miso, caster sugar and mirin in a saucepan and simmer over low heat for about 5 minutes. Remove from the heat and add mustard, then mix well. Cool down.
2 Blanch broccoli in salted water for 3–4 minutes. Then cool quickly in iced water. Drain well.
3 In a bowl, combine miso mixture and broccoli.

SERVES 4

120g (4oz) white miso
2 tablespoons caster sugar
1 tablespoon mirin
1 tablespoon wa-garashi
  (Japanese or English mustard)
300g (9½ oz) broccoli, trimmed
Salt, to taste

Note
Instead of broccoli, you could use asparagus, turnip, or rape flowers.

Gōyā
Bitter melon from Okinawa

I had never seen bitter melon 20 years ago, but I am amazed these days that we can see bitter melon throughout Japan in summer.

Nigauri (bitter melon) is called *gōyā* in Okinawa, the southern island of Japan and on the mainland. The fruit has a distinct warty looking exterior and an oblong shape. It is hollow in cross-section, with a relatively thin layer of flesh surrounding a central seed cavity filled with large flat seeds and pith. The flesh is crunchy and watery in texture, similar to cucumber. Bitter melon is rarely used on mainland Japan, but is a significant component of Okinawan cuisine.

Okinawa was once the independent kingdom of Ryúkyú. The islands were annexed by Japan during the Meiji Restoration in 1879 when punitive taxes were imposed and indigenous culture, language and religion were suppressed. Worse was to come during World War II, when heavy bombardment and suicidal Japanese tactics decimated the islands. After the war, they remained under US occupation until 1972. Since then, Okinawa's sub-tropical climate and beautiful ocean, nature and distinct culture have attracted many people. Okinawa has become one of the major tourist destinations for the Japanese.

Recently gōyā was introduced to mainland Japan and has now spread all over because of its rich nutritious element. Bitter melon stimulates digestion but care is needed because while this can be helpful for people with a sluggish digestion, dyspepsia and constipation, it can sometimes make heartburn and ulcers worse.

Other typical Okinawan ingredients include vegetables rarely seen on the Japanese mainland such as *murasaki-imo* (purple yam). Okinawan tropical fruits, including mango, papaya, pineapple, dragonfruit and the sour lime-like *shíkuwāsā* (calamansi), are delicious when in season. *Kurozatō* (dark cane sugar) is also a popular snack, eaten both plain and made into a vast variety of candies and pastries.

ゴーヤちゃんぷる

Gõyã chanpurú

Stir-fried Bitter Melon with Pork and Egg

Chanpurú means 'mixture' in Okinawa (Ryúkyú) language.

1 Wrap tofu in a muslin cloth or kitchen paper, and weigh it down for about 20 minutes to extract the liquid. Tear tofu into pieces with your fingers.

2 Trim off the ends of the gōyā. Cut in half lengthways and scrape out seeds and white pith with a tablespoon. Slice thinly, transfer into a bowl and sprinkle with salt. Knead in the salt with your hands to remove bitterness, rinse thoroughly and drain well.

3 Heat oil and cook the egg over high heat for about 20 seconds, stirring constantly until set like scrambled eggs.

4 Add tofu and pork slices and cook through, stirring fast.

5 Add soy sauce, salt and chilli oil to taste.

6 Serve sprinkled with bonito flakes.

SERVES 4

400g (13oz) momen-dofu (hard tofu)
Salt
400g (13oz) gōyā (bitter melon)
2 tablespoons vegetable oil
2 eggs, beaten
200g (6½ oz) sliced pork
Soy sauce, to taste
Salt, to taste
Chilli oil, to taste
Bonito flakes, to taste

水菜サラダ
Mizuna-sarada
Mizuna with Mustard Soy Dressing

Mizuna (Japanese mustard) is also called kyona in Kyoto. Mizuna is harvested between October and March. The dark glossy green leaves with dandelion-like jagged edges and white stems have a mild, sweet mustardy taste. Mizuna is used in salads, pickles, stir-fries and soups. There is another similar species to mizuna called mibuna. It is better used in cooked dishes such as sukiyaki. Mizuna and mibuna are rich sources of Vitamin C, calcium and iron and can be found in selected vegetable shops.

1 To remove excess oil from the usu-age, place in boiling water and cook for two minutes. Drain and when it has cooled down, squeeze out any water and slice.
2 Boil water in a pan and add salt.
3 Blanch mizuna and drain, then leave it under running water until its cooled down.
4 Drain well and squeeze out water.
5 Mix with mustard, mirin and soy sauce to make mustard dressing.
6 Toss mizuna and usu-age in dressing and garnish with sesame seeds.

1 sheet usu-age (thin deep-fried sliced tofu)
Salt, pinch
400g mizuna or rocket leaves
1 teaspoon hot mustard
2 teaspoons mirin
½ tablespoon light soy sauce
1 tablespoon roasted sesame seeds

SERVES 4

Japanese Versus Western Food

L anguage can be confusing, so I'll explain. Japanese food is called *wa-shoku*. *Wa* means things Japanese and *shoku* is food. *Yo-shoku* is Western food. Regional Japanese food—local crops and fish, as well as meat cooked with traditional local cooking methods, is called *dosandoho-shoku*. Outside Japan, *wa-shoku* is more simply identified as *sushi*, *soba* and *tempura*. *Wa-shoku* today is not necessarily what it was 150 years ago. Since the onset of the Meiji Era (1868), Western foods such as beef and dairy have influenced Japan's eating habits. Many Japanese assume that these foods are traditional *wa-shoku*.

Yo-shoku actually uses Western ingredients or methods, adapted to suit Japanese tastes. *Yo-shoku* is relatively recent, yet is now part of Japanese cuisine. Watching people cook I see this mixture of Japanese and Western food emerging. Ingredients, flavours, seasonings and sauces evolve into something only just recognisable as Japanese. Chicken-rice and *om*-rice have no direct equivalents in the West, *Tonkatsu* (pork cutlets) might resemble schnitzel and *shichu*. Although it sounds like stew, it doesn't look or taste like any stew Westerners know. Japanese curry rice does not taste like Indian or Asian varieties. Hot-pot dishes sometimes include foreign ingredients, such as *kimchi* from Korea. Hamburger has the same name, but may have soy sauce and grated daikon instead of barbecue sauce and salad. It can contain enoki or shiitake mushrooms or Japanese seasonings and be served with rice instead of a bun. Spaghetti may include *mentaiko* (preserved fish roe), *tarako* (cod roe), *nattou* (fermented soy beans), *shiso* (Japanese basil) or even *ume-boshi* (pickled plums), enough to give an Italian a seizure! We call these dishes *wa-shoku*—Japanese-style—and they certainly are, if not of Japanese origin.

New products, new tastes and new cooking methods continue to drive change. Some traditional foods are being abandoned, but people like 83-year-old Mrs Namikawa in Kyoto have started grassroots campaigns to defend traditional cuisine. This wonderful woman still grows Kyoto-style vegetables in her garden for her traditional cooking and customs classes. (see page 92).

Having left Japan so long ago, it is important for me to teach Japanese cuisine wherever I am. When I hear of activities like this, things being handed down from one generation to the next, I feel the same comfort I derive from the sound of a newborn baby crying, an assurance that life goes on.

和風ハンバーガー

Wa-fú Hamburger

Hamburger with Mushrooms

Wa means Japanese and fú means style so Wa-fú hamburger means hamburger Japanese-style. There are many wa-fú dishes these days where Asian and Western dishes are introduced to Japan then modified into wafú-style dishes using traditional ingredients and methods. When I asked Japanese housewives with teenage children about their favourite dinner menus, this dish was among those at the top of the list.

1 Heat oil in a frying pan and add onion. Stir over medium heat until transparent, then allow to cool.
2 Put beef in a bowl and season with salt, pepper and nutmeg. Mix together with your hands until well combined.
3 Add breadcrumbs or bread to meat and mix well.
4 Stir through egg yolk and onion.
5 Divide the mixture into four oval shapes. Using your thumb, apply pressure in the centre to make a dent. Lay hamburger on an oven tray and grill (broil) until cooked.
6 Just before the hamburgers are cooked, trim and clean the mushrooms. Stir-fry them with the carrot for 1 minute, adding dashi and soy sauce as they cook. Simmer for 30 seconds. Add potato starch mixture and mix to thicken. Add spring onion. Season with ginger.
7 Serve with boiled egg, tomatoes, lettuce and potato salad (see page 111).

SERVES 4

Vegetable oil
1 large brown onion, peeled and chopped
600g (1 ¼ lb) minced (ground) lean beef
Salt and pepper, to taste
Nutmeg, to taste
½ cup breadcrumbs or 1 piece of white bread, soaked in ½ cup (125ml/4fl oz) milk
1 egg yolk
mushrooms to taste, such as enoki, eringe, shimeji
½ carrot, peeled and cut into match sticks
1 cup (250ml/8fl oz) dashi, warm
1 teaspoon soy sauce
½ tablespoon potato starch, mixed with ¼ cup (60ml/2fl oz) dashi
1 spring onion stem, sliced
1 teaspoon ginger juice
Boiled egg
Cherry tomatoes
Lettuce leaves

ポテトサラダ

Poteto sarada

Potato Salad

This type of potato salad is quite popular in Japan. It can be used in sandwiches or lunch-boxes or eaten with hamburgers.

1 Slice cucumber thinly, sprinkle with salt and then rub it in. Squeeze to remove excess liquid.
2 Mix cucumber with the potatoes, ham, egg and vegetables. Add mayonnaise and season with salt and pepper.

SERVES 4

1 cucumber

Salt

4 medium potatoes,
    cooked, peeled and mashed

2–3 slices ham, chopped

1 hard boiled egg, chopped

⅓ cup frozen vegetables
    (such as corn, green peas,
    carrots), defrosted and cooked

⅓ cup (80ml/2½fl oz)
    Japanese mayonnaise

Salt, to taste

Pepper, to taste

Breakfast

Breakfast was born in Japan towards the end of World War II. American soldiers landed and controlled the Japanese government, westernising the eating habits of the Japanese. Bread, butter and milk, for example, were introduced. I remember such foods didn't suit my tastes, but I was very interested in them.

During my childhood in the 1950s, we had steamed rice, miso soup, pickles and newly laid eggs for breakfast at home. At that time we had six hens in a small chicken coop, about three square metres in size. Also during that time in our house we used a *makigama* (an old cast-iron cooking pot). We were a big family and I remember every morning we used to cook the rice in a huge okama (pot). We used to eat a lot of plain rice every day and sometimes we also ate mixed rice such as imo-gayu (with sweet potato) and oka-yu (goulash) and steamed rice mixed with wheat.

Since then the Japanese breakfast has changed a lot. We now have very convenient kitchen utensils and facilities, for example automatic rice cookers, toasters and coffee makers. Most Japanese people these days love bread, butter, jam, cheese, cereal, milk, coffee and juice. I think people don't want to spend the time to prepare traditional Japanese breakfasts any more. Also some people do not eat breakfast at all. While travelling in Japan you can choose either Japanese or Western-style breakfasts at *ryōkan* or hotels.

Later in the 1960s, grocery shops and supermarkets started to sell fresh eggs. Eventually we lost our hens from our chicken coop and my big brother started to keep pet pigeons in the chicken coop instead. Early in the morning we children would be woken to the sound of our mother chopping vegetables on the chopping board. Always at that time we would hear the sound of a vendor selling tofu and *nattou* (fermented soy beans), who would play the flute around the streets as he passed by. My job was to run and buy tofu from him.

Breakfast Recipes

Ganmodoki (page 67) Tofu Miso Soup (page 68), mizuria salad, cooked soy beans, seasoned nori sheets, pickles, cooked rice.

Lunch

When I travel in Japan, I always enjoy lunch, whether it is the casual atmosphere, the low prices or the special lunch menus, I cannot say, maybe the combination of all three. I find the set menus in regular restaurants just as tempting as the fine dining menus in upmarket establishments. I love the fact that a drink, dessert and usually miso soup are included in the set lunch. Even the *bento*-box at train stations is a wonderful lunch. It is quite an experience to pick up an *ekiben* at stations along your route and sample some regional fare.

At home, most people go for easy-to-prepare lunches such as noodles or use up leftovers in dishes such as fried rice. Working people may take their own *bento*-box, eat in small restaurants or have takeaway delivered to their workplace. Large companies frequently have canteens where employees can eat great meals at very reasonable rates. Most primary schools provide lunch for their pupils, organised by a lunch committee in conjunction with a nutritionist, prepared by licensed cooks and served by students—appropriately gloved and masked—in the classrooms. There has recently been controversy about school lunches. Some people want there to be more freedom of choice or parents want to provide different meals for their children. Others object to children eating in the classrooms. Senior students and those at university typically eat in a canteen.

The history of school lunches is interesting, dating back to the 1940s when two million students in six metropolitan areas were allocated free lunches. At that time only miso soup and rice were provided to the lucky children in these areas. The scheme was interrupted by World War II, but resumed in 1947 when the postwar committee of American soldiers, LARA (Licensed Agency for Relief in Asia), offered school lunches to infant students in metropolitan schools. Later, UNICEF provided skim milk, and bread was provided in 1950 when America started sending flour to Japan. It's hard to imagine that back then bread, not ric, was the staple food for school lunches. Rice, however, was still in short supply following the war. Later, a government-appointed body distributed any excess rice to schools as part of the school lunch program. Eventually, in 1976, the government decided to supply white polished rice to all school children for lunch as part of their program to promote the consumption of rice. In 1990, food education came under the spotlight throughout Japan and many communities instituted food education programs promoting good practices in eating, with the emphasis on a balanced diet and a choice of local ingredients in their school lunch programs.

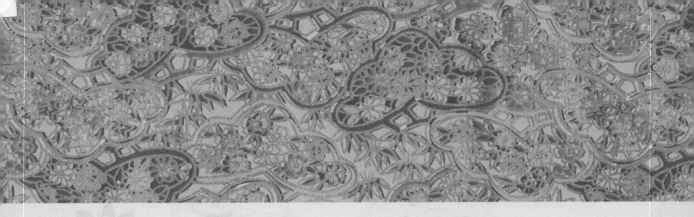

Dinner

Dinner at home used to be the most exciting family gathering but nowadays it seems that everyone is too busy to get together around the table for a convivial family dinner.

Preparation for the dinner was traditionally a woman's job. After finishing the housework she would visit the shops to buy the ingredients. In our family, I usually had to do the shopping for the evening meal and I remember the dusty streets with some nostalgia. They were alive with everyone's daily trips to the butcher, vegetable and fruit shops, fish shop and deli as the vital foods for the evening meal were acquired in the late afternoon. Of course, if I think about it, this was only natural, as refrigerators and freezers were not commonplace then and neither were supermarkets. Things started to change round the seventies, when supermarkets became more prevalent and people were both able to shop in more convenient locations and stock up on food. Food shopping has changed again in more recent times as lifestyles have changed and as different foods become available.

It may surprise Westerners to know that family eating patterns in Japan have become more Westernised and that even the once omnipresent rice is eaten less often than it used to be. Bread has finally made an inroad onto Japanese tables and the readily available takeaway Western dishes such as pastas, quiches and salads have become tempting alternatives to the traditional *sushi* and *sashimi* meals for the busy mother to pick up on her way home from work. Consommé and potage frequently replace miso and stock cubes have become a trendy substitute for soy sauce. With the advent of family restaurants, busy families eat out more often, not only for the convenience, but also because mothers are bowing to the tastes of the children rather than the father.

Some families still enjoy traditional Japanese dinners, but many resort to buying them ready-made or have quick and easy stir-fries of vegetables with beef, pork and chicken, though grilled fish remains popular. Unfortunately, with the abundance of delicious pre-prepared foods that are so easily available, many mothers these days are losing the basic culinary skills such as filleting *sashimi*. Why make it yourself when you can buy it?

Dressed Broccoli
with Mustard Miso

Vinaigrette Chicken

Green tea

Cooked rice

Pickles

Daikon and
Beancurd Miso Soup

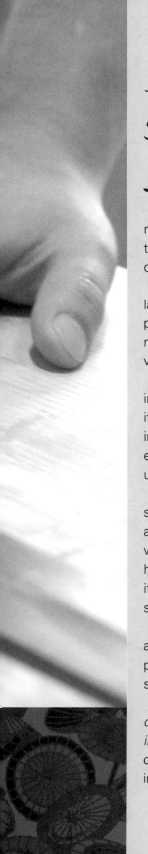

すし
Sushi

The origins of *sushi* date back to Asia in the 4th century BC, when people preserved fish by removing the internal organs, pickling, heavily salting and naturally fermenting it in rice, which extended its shelf life. After a few months the fish was taken out of the rice to eat and the rice was discarded. This was called *nare-zushi* and came to Japan in the Heian Era of the 8th century.

The Japanese invented *namanare-zushi*—fish and rice eaten together, in the late Muromachi Era. *Sushi* changed from being a neccesity to food eaten for pleasure such as *haya-zushi* (box *sushi*) of the Edo Era (1603–1867), vinegar was mixed into the rice without waiting for natural fermentation and vegetables and various dried ingredients were used as well as fish. This style is still seen today.

In early 19th-century central Tokyo (Edo) a street-food industry emerged, including open-air *sushi* bars. This *sushi* had a great reputation all over Tokyo for its sensational taste and convenience. Tokyo-style seaweed rolls are best eaten immediately after being made. The seaweed is roasted to make it crisp and enhance the flavour, then quickly rolled up. Osaka-style seaweed rolls using unroasted seaweed, are rolled tightly and mainly consumed later.

To make *edomae-zushi*, place a piece of fish in the left hand. Lightly hold a small amount of *sushi* rice in the right hand. With the right index finger, pick up a small amount of wasabi and place it on the fish. Place *sushi* rice on to the wasabi and indent it with the left thumb, turn the *sushi* over a few times in the hand, continuously shaping the *sushi* around the indentation and finally closing it over. Do not compress the rice too tightly. The finished forms are straw-bag shape, box shape or ship shape, which is the most popular for *sushi* chefs.

The real pleasure in *edomae-zushi* is combining skill and ingredients to create a great taste sensation—and show off the chef's techniques. Train *sushi* is also popular. *Sushi* robots make the rice balls and ingredients are placed on top and served to guests. It is a very different concept to handmade *nigiri-zushi*.

Varieties of *sushi* include: *nigiri-zushi* (finger *sushi*), *maki-zushi* (rolled in nori), *chirashi-zushi* (scattered), *oshi-zushi* (box), *nare-zushi* (fermented *sushi*) and *inari-zushi* (bean-curd). *Temaki-zushi* (hand rolls) and other individual *sushi*, like cross-over *sushi* combining Western ideas or other Asian ingredients have been introduced, but I hope the traditional *edomae-style* of *sushi* will never change.

細巻き

Hoso maki

Slender Rolls

This is the basic method for rolling up sushi (right-handed). Once you master this, try large rolls and inside-out rolls.

1 Place a bamboo mat on a board or other dry, flat surface.
2 Place half a sheet of nori on the mat, rough side up, one edge of the nori lining up with the front edge of the mat.
3 Dip your right fingers into the vinegar water. With damp fingers, take sushi rice and spread evenly over ⅔ of the nori, leaving a space at the back edge. With your right index finger, draw a line of wasabi along the rice.
4 Place strips of cucumber side by side along the wasabi line.
5 Using both hands, lift the front edge of the mat and roll up to the end of the rice. While still wrapped, gently shape the roll, pushing rice in at both ends with your fingertips.
6 Keep lifting up the front edge of the bamboo mat as you roll the sushi onto the remaining uncovered portion of nori, giving a final light press on the edge before removing the mat completely.
7 With a wet knife, slice the roll in half, then into thirds.
8 Serve with pickled ginger garnish and a dipping dish of soy sauce.

MAKES 6 PIECES

1 nori sheet, halved crossways
Te-zu (vinegar water—1 cup of water combined with 1 teaspoon rice vinegar)
1 cup sushi rice (page 89)
Wasabi paste
¼ Lebanese cucumber, cut lengthwise, seeded and cut into long thin sticks
Pickled ginger, optional
Salt-reduced soy sauce

Note
Spread rice with wet fingers, but be careful not to splash the nori.

For your first attempts at making sushi, keep fillings to a minimum for ease of rolling.

For more variety, you can make sushi using other fillings such as cooked carrot sticks and asparagus.

はだかまき

Hadaka maki
Inside-out Rolls

1 Place nori on the bamboo mat. Wet fingers with te-zu and spread rice all over the nori.
2 Spread a piece of plastic wrap over the rice.
3 Place one hand on top of the plastic wrap, one hand underneath the mat and gently turn upside down. Remove the mat and place it underneath. The resulting arrangement now has the bamboo mat on the bottom, then the plastic wrap, rice and nori on top. With your finger, draw a thin line of wasabi and mayonnaise along the nori. Place salad leaves along the centre of the nori. Place the prawns and asparagus along the central area of the salad leaves.
4 Using dry hands, roll up about two-thirds of the way.
5 Lift the mat and pull free the edge of the plastic wrap so it doesn't get caught in the roll. Roll the last bit up and remove the mat but not the plastic.
6 With a sharp wet knife, cut in half and then quarters, making 8 pieces. Remove the plastic wrap. Decorate with sesame seeds.

MAKES 8 PIECES

1 sheet nori
Te-zu (vinegar water—1 cup of water combined with 1 teaspoon rice vinegar)
1½ cups sushi rice (page 89)
Wasabi paste
1 tablespoon Japanese mayonnaise
2 green salad leaves such as baby cos lettuce
2 large king prawns, cooked, peeled and deveined
2 stems of asparagus, cooked, lower portion removed
Roasted white sesame seeds, for decoration

Note
Other ingredients suitable for toppings are roasted black sesame seeds, tobikko (flying fish roe) and egg mimosa (made by passing the yolk of a hard-boiled egg through a sieve).

てまり寿司

Temari-zushi

Ball-shaped Sushi with Pickled Vegetables

1 To make instant pickles, slice vegetables, then gently
   rub in the salt. Add sliced kelp, chilli and keep in a sealed
   container for a couple of hours or overnight, depending
   on the texture you prefer.

2 To make the sushi, lay a sheet of plastic wrap on
   the bench and place pickles in the centre. Using a
   moistened spoon, scoop up sushi rice and place on
   the top of the pickled vegetables.

3 Draw the edges of the plastic wrap over the rice
   and pickle. While twisting together, shape into a ball.
   Repeat with all the ingredients.

4 Just before serving, remove plastic wrap and decorate
   with nori threads.

SERVES 4

4 thin slices of peeled daikon,
   cut across the length.

4 thin slices of carrot, cut along
   the length of the carrot

8 stems mizuna (Japanese water
   cress) leaves

Salt to taste

1 kelp sheet (approximatley
   10cm (4ins) square), sliced
   into thin strips

1 dry or fresh chilli, de-seeded

4 cups of sushi rice
   (see page 89)

Cabbage or Chinese cabbage

Cucumber

4 slices yellow pickled
   daikon (see note)

4 myoga (Japanese ginger)
   pickles (see note)

Note
Pickles are available from
Japanese grocery shops.

にぎり寿司

Nigiri-zushi

Hand-moulded Sushi from Masa-zushi in Otaru

As you are serving raw prawn flesh, it is important to use sashimi-quality prawns.

1. To prepare prawns, remove heads and shells, but leave tails intact. Devein then make a slit on the belly side to open up like a butterfly. Gently flatten out.
2. Cut slices of tuna and kingfish fillet along the grain to make pieces 6cm long x 2.5cm wide (2½ ins x 1in) and 0.3cm (⅙ in) thick.
3. Moisten your hand with the te-zu and pick up about 1 tablespoon of rice. Form into a rectangular-shaped ball, press gently with the hand but do not squash. Pick up a sushi slice with your other hand and spread on a dab of wasabi with one finger of the hand holding the rice.
4. Place rice on the sushi slice and, with index and middle fingers, press firmly to form a mounded shape. Roll sushi over and press again with two fingers against the fish. Rotate sushi 180 degrees and press again with two fingers against the fish. Place on a plate.

SERVES 4

8 green king prawns, sashimi quality
8 large white scallops, sashimi quality
200g (6½ oz) tuna fillet, sashimi quality
Te-zu (vinegar water—1 cup of water combined with 1 teaspoon rice vinegar)
200g (6½ oz) kingfish fillet, sashimi quality
4 cups sushi rice (see page 89)
Wasabi, to serve
Soy sauce, to serve

巻き寿司

Maki-zushi

Sushi Roll

There are many varieties of fillings for sushi rolls. This is a sushi roll with shigureni (tasty beef).

To make beef (Shigureni):

1 Sprinkle beef with a little sake.
2 Heat up a pan, put in beef and stir for a minute.
3 Add caster sugar, dashi, sake, soy sauce and mirin.
4 Bring to the boil, occasionally removing scum, then add ginger.
5 Cook until almost all the liquid has evaporated. Allow to cool.

300g beef, thinly sliced
Sake, few drops
2 tablespoons caster sugar
1 cup (250ml/8fl oz) bonito dashi
½ cup (125ml/4fl oz) sake
¾ cup (190ml/6fl oz) soy sauce
2 tablespoons mirin
30g (1oz) ginger, peeled
and julienned

MAKES 4 ROLLS

To make roll:

1 Place nori on the bamboo mat rough side up, one edge of the nori lining up with the front edge of the mat.
2 Dip your right fingers into the vinegar water. Take sushi rice and spread evenly over the nori leaving 2cm (¾ in) space at the back edge.
3 Place fillings along the centre in a line.
4 Using both hands, lift the front edge of the mat and roll up to the end of the rice. While still wrapped, gently shape the roll, pushing rice in at both ends with fingertips.
5 Keep lifting up the front edge of the bamboo mat as you roll the sushi on the remaining uncovered portion of nori, giving a final light press on the edge before removing the mat completely.
6 With a wet knife, slice the roll in half, then into thirds.

4 nori sheets
Te-zu (vinegar water—1 cup
of water combined with
1 teaspoon rice vinegar)
6 cups sushi rice (see page 89)
1 egg omelette, cut into strips
(see page 192)
1 Lebanese cucumber,
cut lengthwise, de-seeded
and cut into long thin sticks

Where can you eat sushi?

Would you like to try *sushi* at a *sushi* bar? The Japanese word for *sushi* restaurant is *sushi-ya*. These days, we can have reasonably priced *sushi* at casual restaurants or takeaway shops while eating at a *sushi-ya* is a bit expensive, even for the Japanese. For the beginner, try a *sushi-ya* with a menu with prices; some have no menu and you might get a nasty surprise when you get the bill! However, price is no indicator of quality, so how can we choose? It is fun to sit at the counter and order directly from the chef; count the number of Japanese sitting at the *sushi* bar because the more Japanese people eating there, the better the *sushi*. Japanese people are manic about the quality of *sushi* so asking them where they go to eat is a safe way. Once you find one or two good places, stick to those; regulars get better *sushi* and better overall service than casual patrons.

These days, conveyor-belt *sushi* is very popular; you sit at a counter and make your selections from a revolving conveyor belt; it's fun and inexpensive.

Mr Takayuki Nakamura, Itamae-san, chef at Masazushi in Otaru, Hokkaido

Edomae-*zushi* was originally made with ingredients from Tokyo Bay or nearby, but it is getting hard to get local ingredients these days. Once young apprentices from all over Japan gathered in Tokyo to learn how to make *edomae-zushi* before returning to their home town to open *sushi* restaurants using their own local ingredients. Otaru, Hokkaido (Northern Island) is known as 'the city of Sushi'. It's famous for *sushi*, uses the local fresh ingredients and has more than a hundred *sushi* restaurants.

I tasted *nigiri* made by Mr Nakamura, a young smart *sushi* chef wearing an impressive clean uniform. He told me about their *sushi* and ingredients across the counter as he was working with a *sushi* knife. He held *sushi* rice and a topping, his motion was quick but elegant without being confusing and his arm stretched to serve pieces of *sushi* on a plate in front of me with a smooth constant rhythm. I had *ootoro* (one of the best parts of belly side of tuna), *hokki-gai* (clams), salmon roe and snow crab. It was all so superb.

These are varieties of *Nigiri-zushi* (hand-moulded *sushi*):

O-toro	tuna belly
Maguro	tuna
Hamachi	kingfish
Sake	salmon
Ika	squid
Ebi	prawn
Hotate-gai	scallop
Tai	snapper
Tako	octopus
Ikura	salmon roe
Uni	sea urchin roe
Unagi	(grilled/broiled) freshwater eel
Anago	(grilled/broiled) sea eel
Katsuo	bonito

129

Wasabi

Wasabi is a 'must have' condiment for *sushi* and *sashimi*. *Wasabi* is from the same family as cabbage (*cruciferae brassicae*). Powdered or paste *wasabi* is commonly used overseas, but fresh *wasabi* has a smooth hotness and therapeutic benefits. It has been used as a medicinal herb for more than 1000 years. The best *wasabi*-producing area in Japan is Shizuoka-ken which—at the foot of Mt Fuji and Mt Amagi—is blessed with clear streams and water temperatures between 12–13 degrees. That is why Shizuoka-ken ships premium quality hydroponic *mazuma wasabi* all over Japan.

In Shizuoka-ken Mr Iida, chairman of the Shizuoka-ken Wasabi Union, showed us round Amagi-san's 400-year-old terraced *wasabi* fields. Even in the middle of summer, the cold clear water continuously flows downstream from the foot of the mountain. When I touched the stream, I felt the cool, crisp water and the fresh, green *wasabi* leaves. I found a mature-sized *wasabi* plant by feeling about in the water and slowly pulled it out to avoid damaging the root. Oh! It came out ragged. Then Mr Iida picked a piece of *wasabi* from the field and gave it to me.

Wasabi roots are usually grated. A sharkskin grater is used because if *wasabi* isn't mixed with oxygen the hotness does not develop well. The ridges on sharkskin are fine and rounded producing a smoother grinding effect compared to a metal grater, which is sharp and rough and causes oxidation. *Wasabi*'s heat comes from allyl-isothiocyanate, a chemical compound that is distributed near the skin of the root, so don't peel the skin off before grating. *Wasabi* is volatile and, after it has been grated, it should be covered and not left outside the fridge too long, otherwise it loses its relish. The heat can be toned down by combining it with soy sauce.

The fresh leaves are not wasted either, they are used in *wasabi-zuki,* which is a *wasabi* pickle made by steeping the leaves in sake lees. This, Mr Iida said, is a local speciality in Shizouka-ken. A large variety of *wasabi* products are available today including ice-cream, other cold confectionary and rice crackers (*osenbe, arare*).

Somebody once said, 'We have *sushi*, that's why we have *wasabi*' but we can also say it the other way around, 'We have *wasabi*, that's why we have *sushi*'. Whichever way, *wasabi* and *sushi* are a great combination and as popular today as ever.

Nori

Like *wasabi*, *nori* is an important ingredient in *sushi*. *Nori* had an image problem in the West, many felt it looked and almost tasted like carbon paper but nowadays the situation has changed with *nori* gradually being accepted among people outside Japan through the popularity of *maki-zushi* (*sushi*-rolls) and their convenience as a finger food.

Nori has a long history. In the middle of the Edo Era (1603–1867) it began to be cultivated in Tokyo Bay. Seaweed was laid over bamboo mats and dried in flat sheets using the same techniques used for making *washi* (Japanese paper). The most difficult part in the cultivation was the first stage of seeding. People did not know where and how *nori spore* lived between spring and autumn and there was little knowledge of the ecosystem, so that the seeding process relied on experience. As a result of this, cultivation was not productive and very insecure.

In 1949, an English algae scholar from Manchester University, Dr Kathleen Mary Drew, uncovered the mystery of the life of *nori*. Dr Drew recognised the dark black colour of algae on the surface of oyster shells at the beach, examined it under the microscope and found its shape was threadlike. She went on to establish that *nori* had the same threadlike shape and, as a result of her discovery, Professor Sokichi Segawa, of Kyushu University finally succeeded in artificially seeding *nori*, therefore enabling mass production. Dr Drew passed away in 1957 never knowing the enormous contribution she made to the *nori* industry. A monument in her honour as the saviour of *nori* fishermen was erected in 1963 in Sumiyoshi Shrine Park, Kumamoto and a festival called Drew-sai is held every year on the 14th of April in her honour.

While in Kumamoto I visited the Kawaguchi Fishery Co-operative formed by Mr Fukushima who organised for me to meet *nori* wholesaler, Mr Yoshida and *nori* makers Mr Nakamura and Mr Hashimoto. According to Mr Yoshida, sales are constant despite a drop in both domestic consumption and in the custom of giving packets of *nori* as gifts. This is because sales to convenience stores have increased due to the popularity of *onigiri* (rice balls) and inquiries from overseas chefs who would like to use the authentic Japanese product. According to Mr

Yoshida, the days making *nori-maki* (*nori* roll) on special occasions at home are coming to an end because of the availability of a greater variety of foods. Comparing the popularity of *sushi* at home and overseas, Mr Yoshida said that in Japan, *nigiri-sushi* (hand-moulded *sushi*) at a *sushi* bar is more popular than *nori-maki* (*nori* rolls) whereas overseas, people tend to eat more *nori-maki*. Mr Yoshida is expecting more Kumamoto *nori* will be introduced overseas and he would be happy if everyone was able to get a chance to know and use their wonderful product.

Mr Nakamura and Mr Hashimoto appreciate that Kawaguchi has very good conditions for *nori*. However, because the process is so delicate, any change in conditions can, in a split second, affect the quality, so production is an anxious process. They are dedicated to protecting the local environment. They emphasised the importance of living in harmony with nature and that every sheet of *nori* is a blessing from nature.

There are many types of *nori*, each one has a different colour and taste, including dry *nori*, roasted *nori*, *ao-nori* (green *nori*) and rock *nori*. Dry *nori* has a black glossy colour and a different sea flavour to roasted *nori*, which is why *sushi* chefs prefer it; the varieties are mainly *asakusa-nori* and *susabi-nori*. *Asakusa-nori* is tender and has a good flavour whereas *susabi-nori* has an excellent colour, gloss and sweetness and is thicker so that it is easier to handle. Roasted *Nori* can be used straight away so it is very convenient. Green *nori* is just sprinkled over *okonomiyaki* (pancakes) and *takoyaki* (dumplings). Rock *nori* grows naturally on rocks and belongs to the *ao-nori* family. It is used for *tsuku-dani*, which is preserved food boiled in soy sauce or other seasonings.

菜の花の散らし寿司

Chirashi-zushi

Scattered Sushi with Nanohana

1. Trim nanohana and blanch with a pinch of salt. Drain then soak in iced water until cooled down. Then drain again and squeeze out the excess water with your hands. Cut into 5cm (2in) long pieces.
2. Soak nanohana in bonito stock for about 1 hour.
3. Combine mustard, soy sauce and mirin.
4. Take nanohana out of the stock and place on kitchen paper to drain excess liquid.
5. Add nanohana to the mustard sauce and combine.
6. Place mixture on top of the sushi rice and top with salmon caviar.

SERVES 4

1 bunch of nanohana (canola or rape-flower) stems, cleaned and washed—see note

Salt, pinch

1 cup (250ml/8fl oz) bonito stock, cooled

1 tablespoon Japanese or English mustard

2 teaspoons light-coloured soy sauce

1 tablespoon mirin

4 bowls of cooked sushi rice (see page 89)

⅓ cup (80ml/2½ fl oz) salmon caviar

Oodles of Noodles

When I'm peckish, I love a bowl of noodles. They are so quick and easy to make and there are no strict rules. There are many varieties: *udon, soba* (buckwheat), *chúka-soba* (Chinese noodles), *sōmen* (thin Japanese noodles) and *rāmen* (egg noodles with broth) as well as dried, fresh or frozen with varying degrees of thickness and firmness. The *rāmen* in Sapporo is quite different to that in Tokyo and different again to the *Hakata* (Fukuoka) variety. Noodles originated in China but, like most introduced foods, they have changed to suit Japanese tastes. The Japanese enjoy varieties of *rāmen* depending on the seaon; in summer, they eat cold noodles and warm up with *rāmen* in broth in winter.

It was once common to see *rāmen* stalls in city streets late at night, catering for those out socialising. As far back as the Edo Era (1603–1867) there were *soba* sellers (*yonaki-sobaya-san*) roaming the streets at night, playing a flute called a *charumera* to attact customers. I am told there are still some around but, as their businesses became more successful they bought shops, so maybe that is where they are today and who knows where the *charumera* are! I remember, when I was studying for high school exams late at night, the sound of the flute tempting me to rush out and buy a bowl of *soba* to keep me going, though perhaps it was just a thankful distraction from all that study. You can make a little noise when you eat noodles; it is not considered bad manners.

Udon noodle

Udon are beautiful, fat, white noodles that look like a real meal. Their main ingredient is weak, or medium,138 strength plain flour with salt and water combined to make the dough. It is flattened, sliced and boiled. *Udon* noodles are eaten with a stock of bonito, kelp and soy sauce. In Kansai (Kyoto/Osaka) they use light-coloured soy (*usukuchi Shōyu*), but in Tokyo they use dark soy.

Udon is a popular fast food often eaten as a substitute for rice. Many noodle shops have their own *dashi* (stock) prepared for the day and simply add *udon* or *soba* noodles as requested, for quick service. Even on train platforms you can buy delicious hot *udon* and sit, or often stand, at the counter to eat it. You can't take the food on the train, but don't worry about missing one. They run so frequently there is always another close behind.

きつねうどん

Kitsune-udon

Hot Udon Noodles with Fried Soy Bean Curd

Kitsune udon, originally from Osaka, are eaten in hot broth with spring onion and fried tofu on top. Kitsune means fox, this is because the Japanese people believe that fried tofu is the fox's favourite food. Other types of udon are tempura udon, which is topped with tempura, curried udon, which is in curry sauce and tsukimi udon (literally means full moon), which is topped with a raw egg and a strip of nori.

1 Cut abura-age into triangles. Place in a saucepan with soy sauce, mirin, sugar and dashi, and simmer until abura-age absorbs most of the liquid.
2 Make up dashi soup, add soy sauce and mirin and then bring to a simmer. Add salt to taste.
3 Boil water in another pan and cook udon noodles according to the instructions on the packet.
4 Drain udon and divide among bowls. Pour soup over and top with seasoned abura-age kamaboko, and spring onion.
5 Serve with shichimi.

SERVES 4

4 abura-age (fried soy bean curd), blanched and drained
2 tablespoons soy sauce
2 tablespoons mirin
2 tablespoons caster sugar
½ cup (125ml/4fl oz) dashi soup stock

Soup
6 cups (1½ litres/3½ pints) dashi soup
⅓ cup (80ml/2½ fl oz) light-coloured soy sauce
2 tablespoons mirin
Salt, to taste

4 servings udon noodles
4 slices kamaboko fish cake
2 stems spring onion, trimmed and chopped
Shichimi (Japanese seven spices), for seasoning

Rãmen

After the Second World War, *rãmen* noodles were brought from China by returning soldiers and their families, along with bean sprouts that were served in all sorts of new dishes such as *tanmen* (vegetable *rãmen*)—dishes which now seem like they have been a part of Japanese cuisine forever. It was at that time that dishes like fried rice (*chã-han*) and vegetable stir-fry (*yasai-itame*), *mãbõdõfu* (tofu stew) and *gyõza* (dumplings) also came to Japan.

Typically these thin *rãmen* noodles, either straight or curly, are served in a soup with roasted pork, chopped spring onions and a boiled egg chopped in half, but there is an endless range of combinations, from the quite orthodox Japanese flavours of *Shõyu-rãmen* with a soy based stock and maybe chicken and vegetables added, to those with a very rich pig's trotter stock and added chilli oil, onion, vinegar and black pepper. Fish stock with soy and mirin is a popular combination somewhere in the middle. *Rãmen* dishes may be named after a region where they are popular or after a particular ingredient. *Shi-o rãmen* has extra salt and is maybe more like the original Chinese style. *Miso-ramen*, as the name implies, uses miso in the stock.

If you go to Sapporo, in Hokkaido, you won't miss the fact that *miso-rãmen* originated there, in 1955, as it is very well publicised everywhere. There is a district called Rãmen Yokocho where people queue to go into the many *rãmen* shops and it is a worthwhile experience. The change over to miso from a salty flavour, along with the use of garlic and lard, gave *Sapporo rãmen* its unique identity. Even more unusually, they cook the *rãmen* in with the vegetables and stock, rather than adding the noodles to the prepared stock. They also add corn kernels and butter at the end, unlikely ingredients for traditional Japanese food.

Tonkotsu-ramen (pig's trotter *rãmen*) is so named for its base stock, which gives it a rather unattractive dull colour. However, the flavour is anything but dull. It is especially popular in the southern regions such as Kumamoto, Miyazaki, Kagoshima and Hakata in Kyushu. And more recently, in areas from Tokyo through Yokahama, Okayama and Hiroshima, chefs have been saucing it up with soy, giving it extra colour and flavour. *Tonkotsu rãmen* is particularly popular in Hakata and is consequently often called *Hakata rãmen*. *Hakata rãmen* uses pig's trotter soup with white sesame, mustard cress and a topping of red-coloured ginger. The noodles are very thin, so it cooks in no time at all.

Basic Tokyo *rãmen* is a very simple dish made with soy sauce and chicken or bonito stock. In Tokyo they usually use the curly variety of noodles rather than

the straight and it may include any combination of roasted pork, fish cake, spinach (silverbeet), boiled egg, *nori*, *shinachiku* (Chinese-style preserved bamboo shoots) and chopped spring onions.

Whatever type of noodles you fancy, enjoy eating them in the Japanese way. Both the Chinese and Japanese attack the noodles with chopsticks, but the Chinese use renge—a spoon—to eat the soup. These days, this manner is used to eat *rāmen* too, although the Japanese still lift the bowl from the table and drink the soup directly from the bowl. Not only this, it must be remembered that it is totally acceptable to slurp the noodles and the soup. Sucking up the noodles from the chopsticks allows you to eat a good mouthful at a time, the best way to enjoy such a fulfilling dish.

札幌味噌ラーメン

Sapporo Miso Rãmen
Rãmen Noodles in Sapporo Style

1 To make miso paste for the soup, use a food processor to whiz onion, carrot and garlic. Heat chilli oil and sesame oil in a frying pan and lightly stir-fry the vegetables. Add soy sauce, sake and caster sugar, and miso, and stir until well combined.

2 Cook egg noodles according to the instructions on the packet and drain.

3 In the meantime, heat up the chicken stock and add miso-paste.

4 Stir in cabbage, pork and fungus and season with pepper.

5 Transfer noodles into each bowl and pour in the soup, then sprinkle over whichever toppings you like.

SERVES 2

Miso Soup

1 onion, peeled
1 carrot, peeled
1 clove garlic
Chilli oil, few drops
1 teaspoon sesame oil
¼ cup (60ml/2fl oz) soy sauce
1 tablespoon sake
1 teaspoon caster sugar
¼ cup (60ml/2fl oz) miso
2 portions of egg noodles
1 litre (1¾ pints) chicken stock
    (preferably make stock from
    chicken bones, but you may
    use a chicken stock cube)
4 leaves of cabbage, chopped
20g (½ oz) thinly sliced pork
    or minced (ground) pork
1 tablespoon black fungus
(available from Asian grocers),
    soaked in water and drained
White pepper, to taste

Optional Toppings

1 tablespoon roasted
    sesame seeds
4 stems of spring onion
    or shiraganegi (Japanese-style
    spring onion), sliced thinly and
    soaked in water
Bean sprouts
Garlic chives
Nori

ひやし中華

Hiyashi-chúka

Cold Noodles with Vinaigrette Soup

This is reimen, a cold noodle dish I had in Yamagata. You can serve with gomadare (spicy sesame sauce) instead of the mustard.

1 To prepare soup, place chicken stock, soy sauce, rice vinegar and sugar in a saucepan, then bring to the boil. Remove from the heat and add sesame oil.
2 Cook egg noodles following the directions on the packet, drain and rinse under running water.
3 Prepare as many toppings as you like.
4 Serve noodles with toppings and mustard. Sprinkle with sesame seeds.

SERVES 4

1 cup (250ml/8fl oz) chicken stock
⅓ cup (80ml/2½ fl oz) soy sauce
¼ cup (60ml/2fl oz) rice vinegar
1 tablespoon caster sugar
2 teaspoons sesame oil
4 portions of egg noodles
English mustard, to serve
1 tablespoon roasted sesame seeds

8 cherry tomatoes, rinsed
8 grapes, rinsed
2 tablespoons menma (pickled bamboo shoot), sliced
½ carrot, peeled and sliced into thin sticks
1 tablespoon cooked corn

Note
Optional Toppings
4 eggs, lightly fried as a very thin omelette and sliced
2 Lebanese cucumbers, cut into quarters lengthways, de-seeded and sliced
8 slices leg ham, chopped
8 dried shiitake mushrooms, rinsed and soaked in a cup (250ml/8fl oz) of water, stems discarded and cooked with 1 teaspoon soy sauce, 1 tablespoon mirin and ½ teaspoon caster sugar, then drained and sliced

Soba

Soba are thinnish, light brown noodles made with a combination of buckwheat and plain flour. Proportions vary from one region to another, as do the cooking methods. They may be served simply with a dipping sauce of soy sauce and bonito stock, called *zarusoba*, or cooked in a variety of dishes served hot or cold, such as *tempura-soba*.

New Year is a time of special celebration in Japan and one lasting tradition is for the family to get together on New Year's Eve and eat bowls of *toshikoshi-soba* while listening to *jo-ya-no-kane* (108 bell chimes) wafting through the air from the local shrine. It is said this custom evolved in the middle of the Edo Era (1603–1867) and because noodles are long, they represent long life and there is no better time to wish and pray for long life than on New Year's Eve. Another theory is that in the Edo Era, goldsmiths used *soba-dango*, balls of soba, to pick up the small fragments of gold from the floor. Consequently it was considered an omen of good fortune to eat soba. Whatever the case, it is certainly an enjoyable way to spend New Year's Eve.

Soba Dõjõ

Normally people do not associate the word *dōjō* with a cooking school. Westerners would most certainly think of a *dōjō* as a place where any of the Japanese martial arts are taught. In Japan, it covers any physical training facility, including professional wrestling schools. More recently, the meaning of the term has expanded to include schools of other artistic pursuits as well.

On a recent trip to Japan, I discovered a *soba dōjō* in a small town in the western part of Saitama Prefecture. I was told that such a school is not only for learning soba-making techniques, but can be considered as a place for developing self-discipline, which makes you wonder whether there is a lot more to soba making than you first imagined!

I approached my challenge at the Arakawatatei soba dōjō with this in mind. This is a school managed by the Japan Agricultural Co-operative Association in Chichibu, Saitama, only 90 minutes by Seibu Railway from Ikebukuro, Tokyo. Chichibu is in a scenic mountainous area, much of which is designated as a National Prefectural Park. About 87 per cent of Chichibu's area is forest and it is a popular district for hiking. Being a mountainous region with poor soil quality, it is not suitable for rice cultivation, but *sericulture* (silk production) has been a thriving industry for some time. I learned, however, from a teacher at the school, that the mountain terrain and poor soil are no hindrance to the growth of buckwheat, which will apparently grow like a weed. Most of the teachers are local old ladies and farmers not in the soba business. The ladies did not learn all about soba from textbooks, but from their mothers-in-law when they first married and came to live in the district. I was very impressed by their knowledge and found that even with my experience, there is always something new to learn about soba.

Making Soba

This is the method we used at the Arakawatei soba dōjō. You will need a large, shallow wooden mixing bowl, (maybe an old salad bowl) and a very long rolling pin. If you don't have one, you can divide the dough into two or three portions and roll them separately.

The ratio of soba, buckwheat flour and plain flour can be changed depending on your preference. However, add too much soba flour and it gets harder to make a dough.

1 Sift flours together and add water in three equal amounts, mixing gently between additions using both hands. As the water is incorporated, the dough gradually clumps together. Continue to mix into one large ball. Knead until the dough becomes glossy. At this stage the ball is still not yet smooth and even.

2 Using the palm of your hand, knead the dough ball against the side of the bowl for about ten minutes until the surface becomes smooth, even and glossy.

3 Transfer the dough onto a large floured board or bench top.

4 Taking care not to tear the outer edges, flatten the ball from the centre outwards with your hands to make a large circle. Sprinkle some flour on top of the dough and use a rolling pin to roll the dough from the centre out in all directions to a distance of about 1cm (½ in) from the edge. It is important not to roll right to the edge so that it doesn't split. When the dough is about 40cm (16ins) in diameter and about 1cm (½ in) thick, sprinkle it with flour. Place the rolling pin towards the edge of the circle and gently roll the dough on to the pin, making sure it is securely rolled. Flour the board again, then gently and evenly roll the pin backwards and forwards and from side to side along the length of the pin, making sure the dough is being pressed evenly. Repeat this 4 or 5 times, until the dough is very thin.

300g (9½ oz) soba (buckwheat flour)
200g (6½ oz) plain flour
200–230ml (6–8fl oz) water —you may need more or less water depending on the weather conditions and humidity. You need to look at the dough and adjust the amount accordingly.
Extra plain flour, for dusting

5 Flour the board once more. Unroll the dough onto the board and sprinkle more flour on the top. Fold the dough in half, sprinkle with flour, fold in half again in the same direction, each time supporting the edges with both hands so that the dough doesn't break.

6 Using a long blade knife, slice across the folded dough to a thickness of 1–1.5mm (½ ins) pushing the knife away from the body, not towards it. This should be enough to make 4 portions of approximately 150g (5oz) each.

7 Note that the whole cooking process should take no more than 40–50 seconds.

8 Bring a large saucepan of water to the boil and lower the noodles in, separating them with your fingers as you do so. When the noodles float to the surface, add 100ml (3fl oz) cold water and the noodles will sink. When they rise to the surface again, quickly strain the noodles and place them in another pot of iced water. Gently wash the noodles in the water to remove all excess starchiness. The noodles feel slimy at first, but this washes away. Strain once more and rinse under running water to remove the last of the starchy water, or lift them from the iced water with your hands and place them into a strainer to drain.

てんぷら蕎麦
Tempura-soba
Soba with Tempura

1 Cook and drain noodles (see page 149). Serve on a plate or in a bamboo basket.
2 To make dipping sauce, stir dashi and soy sauce together in a small ball.
3 Top with dipping sauce, and serve wasabi and tempura on the side.

SERVES 4

4 portions of soba noodles, dry or fresh

Dipping Sauce
80ml dashi (see page 78)
2 tablespoons light soy sauce

2 tablespoons mirin
Tempura (see page 200)
Wasabi, to taste
4 tablespoons grated radish

Note
Soba may cause an allergic reaction in some people. Be careful if you have symptoms of atopic dermatitis.

Fish Markets

Uoichiba is the Japanese expression for fish markets. There are fish markets in all the regional or major cities, but the market in Tsukiji, Tokyo is the largest in Japan. It is called an uogashi market, which literally means riverside fish, but is more fondly referred to as the stomach of Tokyo, as it supplies not just fish, but much of Tokyo's fresh food needs.

The origin of the market dates back to the Edo Era at the beginning of the 17th century. When the Shōgun Tokugawa Ieyasu opened up the new Shōgunate in Edo (now Tokyo) he called for the fishermen to supply the kitchens of the castle with fish. In return for their donations, they were given the right to catch and sell leftover supplies in the Nihonbashi area, which became the first fish market to operate on a barter system. This developed and continued to flourish until the market was destroyed in the Great Earthquake of 1923. It later re-opened in its current location in Tsukiji.

The present market operates on a wholesale and retail level and is a fascinating place to visit. It is divided into two sections, the outside market, called jyōgai and the inside market, *jyōnai*. The outside market, with all its little shops is open to the general public from mid-morning to late afternoon and as well as fish, it sells all perishable goods, beverages, catering equipment and utensils at very reasonable prices. The inside wholesale market is only accessible to non-traders by means of a conducted tour. It is administered by local government and is open weekdays only, except public holidays. The first auction trade starts at 5am, when the wholesalers come to buy and the pressure is on as they bid by raising a finger iat the various locations on the floor where the fish are sorted in to categories, depending mainly on size.

At 7am, the wholesalers open up their shops around the perimeters of the inside markets, having transferred their purchases from the auction floor and set them up for display. At 8am, proprietors of restaurants and fish shops swarm in to get their first choices. It is the ultimate peak hour for the market and the place becomes frantic with people jostling and bumping into each other. Whenever I go there, the atmosphere, the noise, the smells, the crowds and the piles of slippery fish remind me of the times when my father would take me there in the school holidays and later when I got my driving licence and became his driver. Of course it was nowhere as big then as it is now, but it was such a special treat, as most people didn't have access to the inside market. We would leave home before sunrise, drive through the sleeping city, then arrive suddenly at the brilliantly illuminated market in the midst of a still dark town. First the shrill sounds of Tokyoites shouting at the top of their voices, then the smells of the fish and the sea. With the continual hosing, it was always wet and slippery, so we wore long rubber boots like soldiers. As time went by, I felt like I was really one of the professionals, though at this time I was still doing my basic training to become an *itamae* (chef). I thought I was pretty big time, but I realise now of course that I wouldn't have had this opportunity if it wasn't for the family restaurant. After my father had made his purchases, we would drop into one of the *sushi* shops in the inner market and have a meal. It was there, sitting at the *sushi* counter in the early mornings with my father that I started to appreciate the characteristics of tuna and the blue-skinned aomoon (literally, 'fish with blue skin' such as sardines and mackerel). These are life's treasured moments.

On a recent trip to Japan I was fortunate to visit a number of fish markets throughout the country and was amazed at the fresh local seafood I saw. In regional markets such as Makurazaki in the Port of Kyúshú there were wonderfully fresh yellowfin tuna. In Hakodate, Hokkaido there were mouth-watering pacific snow crabs, squid and calamari, all so beautifully fresh. The tuna in Makurazaki had probably only been caught a few hours before; I imagined I could still hear its heart beat. The flesh was very firm, the eyes sparkling, the tail lustrous. It was in perfect condition to be professionally aged under a strict regime of refrigeration so that it will be at its best in 2–5 days, depending on the size. If the tuna has too far to travel or has been sitting around for a long time after it has been caught it is not suitable to be aged. If you are wondering about the freshness of fish, some basic qualities to look for are sparkling eyes, a firm body, bright red gills and a clean ocean smell.

Some fish varieties are available all year round, but others are seasonal. Here are a few that may appear during specific seasons.

Spring:	spring bonito, spring snapper, hairy crab, yellowtail, tuna, clams
Summer:	pike, conger, eel, jewfish, rockfish, Pacific saury
Autumn:	salmon, lobster, atka mackerel
Winter:	puffer fish, octopus, winter kingfish, Japanese fresh water clam, tilefish

サーモンのテリヤキ

Teriyaki

Teriyaki Salmon

Teriyaki sauce is available from Japanese or Asian groceries or major supermarkets, but you can easily make your own. Instead of salmon, tuna, beef or chicken can be used.

1. To make teriyaki sauce, add all the ingredients in a saucepan and bring quickly to the boil, reduce heat and simmer for 15 minutes.
2. Drop a little oil onto the base of the frying pan and swirl to coat.
3. Place salmon in the pan, fry over moderate heat for one minute each side. Add teriyaki sauce and cook 5 minutes over a low heat.
4. Serve in individual dishes, garnished with salad leaves.

SERVES 2

Teriyaki sauce

1 cup dashi

½ cup soy sauce

2 tablespoons caster sugar

1 tablespoon mirin

1 tablespoon fresh ginger juice
   (made by grating fresh ginger
   and squeezing over a bowl)

1 tablespoon sake

Vegetable oil

2 small salmon pieces

Few green salad leaves,
   to garnish

Note
You can also try marinating in teriyaki sauce before wrapping with foil and cooking on the barbecue.

あじの開き塩焼き

Ajino hiraki, shioyaki
Grilled Salted Yellowtail

1 Using your hand pull out gills of the fish and cut them off.
2 Insert a filleting knife into the head of the fish near the mouth. Move the knife along against the spine towards the tail, taking care not to cut through to the other side. The aim is to cut halfway through the fish so that it can be opened out to form a butterfly fillet. Discard the guts and rinse.
3 Pat dry with paper towels or a kitchen towel.
4 Sprinkle skin with mirin and salt.
5 Grill both sides under medium heat.
6 Serve with daikon and soy sauce and garnish with shichimi or yuzu powder and a lime slice on the side.

SERVES 4

4 x 200g (6½ oz) yellow tail
1 tablespoon mirin
1 tablespoon salt
⅓ cup grated daikon radish
Soy sauce, to serve
Shichimi (Japanese seven spices) or yuzu powder for garnishing.
4 slices lime, to serve

海老とサーモンの刺身

Ebi to sãmon no sashimi
Green Prawns and Salmon Sashimi

As you are serving raw prawn flesh, it is important to use sashimi-quality prawns,

1. Make a tsuma (garnish) using daikon. Traditionally it is prepared by peeling off in a continuous sheet and slicing. However, for the novice, use a vegetable peeler or Japanese-style slicer to slice off thin daikon strips. Roll up and cut into thin julienne. Then soak in water until used.

2. To make cucumber tsuma, slice off the skin and roll up, then cut into thin julienne. Soak in water until used.

3. To prepare the prawns, firstly remove the heads and set them aside. With belly side up, use scissors to cut away a strip of shell along the length of the prawn to allow you to lift out the body of the prawn with your finger, taking care not to break the shell.

4. Rinse the heads and shells, and cook in boiling water until they become red. Drain and cool down.

5. Drain daikon and cucumber tsuma well, and serve on individual trays.

6. To slice salmon, trim and cut salmon block to a 2.5cm by 5cm (1 x 2ins) rectangular block. Slice into 0.7cm (⅓ in) thick slices, cutting against the grain. Place on the daikon.

7. For the king prawns, put the flesh back into the shell and arrange on the cucumber with its head.

8. Serve with soy sauce and wasabi.

SERVES 4

200g (6½ oz) daikon radish
1 Lebanese cucumber
8 sashimi-quality green king prawns
400g (13oz) sashimi-quality salmon fillet
Soy sauce for serving
⅓ cup wasabi paste or powder
4 lemon slices, to serve
4 sprigs shiso

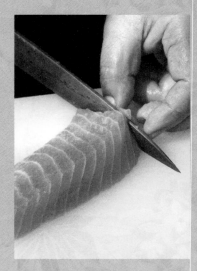

西京焼き

Saikyo yaki

Grilled Spanish Mackerel with White Miso

1 Cut sawara fillet into 4 pieces.

2 Lay fish on a tray and sprinkle with sake.

3 In a bowl, combine miso, mirin and caster sugar.

4 Coat mackerel with miso mixture and refrigerate overnight. For a lighter taste, just set aside for a couple of hours.

5 With a muslin cloth, pat sawara to remove miso.

6 Grill on both sides until lightly scorched. Serve hot garnished with sprigs of kinome or spring onion.

SERVES 4

600g (1 ¼ lbs) sawara fillet
(Spanish mackerel)

1 tablespoon sake

200g (6½ oz) saikyo miso
(white miso)

1 tablespoon mirin

50g (2oz) caster sugar, optional

4 sprigs kinome or spring onion
for garnish

はまぐり

Hamaguri

Clams

1. To remove any sand in the clams, soak in 1litre (1¾ pints) of water and 30g (1oz) salt for about 3 hours with a lid on. Then scrub with a brush and rinse again.
2. Place hamaguri in a large pan and put a lid on. Cook over a low heat for approximately 8 minutes until shells are opened. If there are any unopened ones, discard these. Sprinkle with sake and soy sauce and cook for another a minute. Then sprinkle with mitsuba and yuzu and serve.

SERVES 4

8 hamaguri clams
2 tablespoons sake
2 tablespoons soy sauce
4 mitsuba leaves (Japanese wild chervil) with stem, chopped
1 teaspoon yuzu (Japanese citrus) zest or powder

はまぐりのお吸い物

Hamaguri no osuimono

Clam Soup

1. To remove sand, soak clams in 1 litre (1¾ pints) of water and 30g (1oz) salt for about 3 hours with a lid on. Then scrub with a brush and rinse again.
2. To make a kelp stock, wipe sheet with a dry cloth and soak in 3 cups (750ml/1⅕ pints) water for 30 minutes. Then cook for 2 minutes and take out kelp.
3. Cook hamaguri in a pan over moderate heat for approximately 8 minutes until shells open, removing scum occasionally with a ladle. Add sake, soy sauce and salt. Remove from the heat and serve with mitsuba.

SERVES 4

8 hamaguri clams
1x3cm (1¼ in) kelp sheet
1 tablespoon sake
1 tablespoon light coloured soy sauce
Salt, to taste
4 stems mitsuba (Japanese wild chervil) leaves for garnish

Wagyu

The Meiji Era from 1872, was the opening up of Japanese civilisation to the West. People really began to eat beef at that time, even the Emperor. The Japanese farmers started cross-breeding original Japanese and foreign-bred cattle. Four breeds of beef cattle such as Black, Brown, Shorthorn and No Horn breeds were hybridised to produce a fifth breed called Wagyu.

Wagyu is a breed name, it does not mean Japanese domestic beef. Japanese cows were used as a labour force; their bodies were smaller to make it easier to move around in the rice fields. Since interbreeding with foreign breeds, their bodies are now bigger and the flesh is delicately marbled. Wagyu's flesh is refined and has a tender texture that suits the Japanese delicate palate and sense of the visual. It has a high, even fat content, smoothly melting at a low temperature. You can enjoy the lusciousness of taste melting on the tongue. Wagyu take time to grow into beef cattle and the raising is rather delicate and difficult for mass production and as a result the meat is very expensive.

Farmers started to sell wagyu under the special name of *hida-gyu* in Gifu-ken approximately 20 years ago. To be called *hida-gyu*, the cattle must be kept more than 14 months in Gifu-ken and only include authorised portions of meat, which are graded between grade 3 and 5 by the Japanese Beef Cattle Grading Association. There is a different grading score for marbling. *Hida-gyu* is heavily marbled, soft pink in colour and very tender because the nerve fibres are quite thin. It is said to have a natural sweetness and is therefore very popular for *sukiyaki*, *shabu shabu* and *yakiniku*.

I visited the Gifu-ken Stock Breeding Research Centre where the gap in temperature between the cold winters and hot summers is very great and there is a rich abundance of spring water from the Northern Japanese Alps. This helps to create tender and flavoursome meat. Moreover, feeding the cattle in a wide range of temperatures means there is an increase of saturated fatty acids in the meat.

すき焼き

Sukiyaki

Sukiyaki in Kanto Style

Sukiyaki is usually eaten from a large pot in the middle of the table.

1 To make sauce, bring sake and mirin to the boil. Then add soy sauce and sugar and stir until sugar is dissolved.
2 Oil a heavy pot or sukiyaki pot. Arrange a few of the ingredients, little by little, not all at the same time, in the pot and pour some of the stock over the top. Simmer.

SERVES 4

Warishta sauce
200ml (6fl oz) sake
300ml (10fl oz) mirin
300ml (10fl oz) soy sauce
⅓ cup caster sugar

Vegetable Oil
500g (1lb) beef, thinly sliced
4 stems spring onion, trimmed and sliced
250g hard tofu, diced
250–300g ito-konnyaku (sliced japanese yam cake) or frozen udon noodles, blanched
¼ hakusai (Chinese cabbage), rinsed and cut into bite-size pieces

牛肉の旨煮

Gyuniku no umani

Beef Steak in Broth

1 Slice the beef into 4 pieces and season with salt.
2 Warm dashi in a pan, add soy sauce, mirin and caster sugar, then set aside.
3 Heat a few drops of vegetable oil in a frying pan and place each steak in the pan one by one and sear both sides.
4 Place steaks in the dashi and simmer for 30 minutes.
5 Pour dashi into individual shallow bowls and place steak in centre of each bowl.
6 Top with flower-shaped daikon and wa-garashi.

SERVES 4

800g (1lb9½ oz) sirloin
   (or eye fillet) steak
Salt, to taste
500ml (16fl oz) dashi
   (see page 78)
120ml (4fl oz) soy sauce
1 tablespoon mirin
100g (3oz) caster sugar
4 mitsuba leaves (Japanese
   watercress)
12 pieces of flower-shaped
   daikon
2 tablespoons wa-garashi
   (Japanese or English mustard)

Note
Use a flower-shaped cutter to cut the daikon into flower shapes.

和牛串焼き

Wagyu-kushiyaki

Skewered Wagyu Steak with Wasabi Miso

1 Mix wasabi, miso and caster sugar and set aside.
2 On each skewer, place 2 pieces of beef and a green onion. Repeat until all the beef is used.
3 Sprinkle sake and salt over the skewers.
4 Drop a little oil on the frying pan and heat up over a moderate heat. Then cook both sides of the meat to your preference.
5 Serve on a small plate topped with wasabi-miso paste and lime wedges.

SERVES 4

Alternatives
As an option, transfer beef onto a baking tray and top with wasabi-miso paste. Using a burner, scorch just over the wasabi-miso paste.

1 teaspoon wasabi paste
80g (3oz) light brown miso
1 tablespoon caster sugar

400g (13oz) wagyu or beef, diced in to 50g (2oz) pieces
4 green onions, halved and trimmed to approximately 10cm (4ins)
1 tablespoon sake
Salt, to taste
Vegetable oil
4 thin lime wedges

Pork

Way back in the Jyōmon Era from around 10,000 BC to 300 BC, Japanese people ate wild boar. There are records of early immigrants from Asia farming boar in the early seventh century—the dawn of the pig-farming industry in Japan. However, when Buddhism arrived, eating meat was banned and pig farming was prohibited for the next 1000 years in Japan, though it was still carried out in the remote mountain areas of Satsuma (now Kyúshu) and Ryuukyuu (Okinawa). In 1385, black pigs were introduced to the islands of Okinawa. These were cooked for special occasions and many pork dishes were developed in Okinawa.

In 1609, Japan started trading with Holland and pork farming was re-established. During the Meiji Era (1867–1912), middle-sized Yorkshire and Berkshire pigs were imported from England. During the 1960s, as Japan became more affluent there was an increase in the demand for pork, so larger breeds: Landrace, Large White, Hampshire and Duroc were introduced from Europe and America. There was a dramatic change from medium to large-size pig farming. Including the Yorkshire and Berkshire, these are the most popular and referred to as the Six Major Brands breeds.

Despite the success of the more recently introduced breeds, the black pig, which goes back to the Satsuma days, has the most delicious meat, but they are difficult to farm and so are not readily available. Despite this, they are being farmed again in Kyushu and are making a comeback throughout Japan.

When I was recently in Kyúshu, I visited a pig farm in Makurazaki, where a type of black pig known as *kagobuta* was being bred. These pigs are fed on the lees from the production of *shouchuu*, an alcoholic beverage made from potatoes, which is the local industry in Makurazaki, as well as leftover fishbone from the bonito factory and sweet potatoes from the farm. The animals grow healthy in a natural environment, which must account for the fine texture, tenderness and crisp, clear palate of the Kagobuta pork.

Of the hundreds of pork dishes developed over the years, probably the most popular are *tonkatsu* (crumbed pork cutlet), *katsudon* (a bowl of rice with a crumbed pork cutlet and egg on top), *nabemono* (hot-pot) and *yakibuta* (spit roast pork).

トンコツ

Tonkotsu (Regional Cuisine from Kagoshima-prefecture)

Japanese Pork Rib Stew in Kagoshima Style

It is said that this dish was originally eaten by the Satsuma-samurai warriors on the battlefield. They put all the ingredients in a large pot and cooked them slowly. Nowadays, a pressure cooker can be used to save time. Tonkotsu-lunch boxes are sold at the Kagoshima station.

1 Heat one tablespoon of oil in a pan over high heat and stir-fry pork until half cooked. Pour shōchú over and cook until evaporated. Then add hot water and skim off any unwanted fat from the surface. Remove pork to a large pot or a pressure cooker.

2 Heat the remaining oil in the pan and stir-fry the garlic and onion over medium heat for a couple of minutes. Add burdock, konnyaku and daikon. Stir over the high heat, until lightly browned.

3 Add dashi and bring to the boil. Add shōchú, mirin and sugar, then with a lid on, cook over low heat for about 1–2 hours or until the pork is tender, occasionally skimming the surface.

4 Combine miso with some liquid from the soup in a cup, then pour into the pot with the ginger. Cook for a further 20 minutes. At the end, add in a few drops of oil to taste. Season with salt.

SERVES 4

2 tablespoons vegetable oil

1kg spare-rib pork

½ cup (125ml/4fl oz) Shōchú (Japanese clear spirit)

½ litre (1¾ pints) hot water

1 garlic clove, chopped

1 medium brown onion, peeled and chopped

200g (6½ oz) burdock

200g konnyaku (Japanese yam cake cut into small triangle shapes)

200g daikon-radish

10 cups (2½ litres/4½ pints) dashi

½ cup (125ml/4fl oz) Shōchú or sake

¼ cup (60ml/2fl oz) mirin

¼ cup black sugar

2 tablespoons shishu (light brown) miso

Salt, to taste

1 tablespoon grated ginger

Sesame or chilli oil, to taste

Optional Ingredients

Turnips, potatoes, boiled eggs, deep-fried tofu or carrots.

とんかつ
Tonkatsu

Japanese-style Pork Cutlet with Miso Sauce

1 To make miso sauce, add miso, mirin and caster sugar to a pan and cook for 2–3 minutes. Add ginger and cook 1 minute, stirring, then set aside.

2 Season pork with salt and pepper. Make a few slits in the pork fat with a knife to prevent the pork shrinking when it's deep fried.

3 Prepare salad ingredients and garnish and transfer to each plate.

4 Place the flour, egg and breadcrumbs in separate bowls in a line. Coat pork with flour, then egg, then breadcrumbs.

5 Heat enough oil for deep frying to 180°C (350°F), or test for readiness by dropping in a sprinkle of breadcrumbs; if they float the oil is hot enough.

6 Deep fry pork until golden brown. Drain well, slice and serve with sauces and cherry tomatoes.

SERVES 4

150g akamiso or hacchō miso (dark brown miso)
4 tablespoons mirin
4 tablespoons caster sugar
1 teaspoon grated ginger

4 pieces pork loin— approximately 150g (5oz) each
Salt, to taste
Cracked black pepper, to taste
8 cabbage leaves, thinly sliced and soaked in water
1 Lebanese cucumber, peeled, then peel sliced
4 lemon slices, halved
4 tablespoons curly parsley
1 cup flour
2 eggs, beaten
3 cups coarse breadcrumbs
Vegetable oil for deep frying
20 cherry tomatoes

豚のから揚げ

Buta no kara-age

Crispy Pork

The pork must be very thinly sliced for this dish. The best solution is to freeze the meat almost solid and then slice or purchase it ready sliced from an Asian butchery or grocery shop.

1 Cut the thin slices of pork into bite-size pieces and place on a plate. Sprinkle over sake and soy sauce and set aside for 10 minutes.
2 Pat pork with a kitchen paper to dry.
3 Mix flour and potato starch. Coat pork with the mixture. Set aside again for 10 minutes.
4 To make sauce, combine soy sauce, sake, mirin, sugar and chilli in a bowl.
5 Heat oil in a frying pan and fry pork and until crispy.
6 Pour over sauce and toss to coat over medium heat.
7 Transfer pork onto plate and serve with green salad and spring onions.

SERVES 4

300g (9½ oz) pork, thinly sliced
1 teaspoon sake
1 teaspoon soy sauce
1 tablespoons flour
2 tablespoons potato starch
1 tablespoon soy sauce
2 teaspoons sake
2 teaspoons mirin
2 teaspoons caster sugar
1 small fresh or dry chilli,
    de-seeded and chopped
1 tablespoon vegetable oil
Green salad
Spring onion, trimmed
    and chopped

餃子

Gyoza

Gyoza Dumplings

1. To prepare dipping sauce, combine all ingredients in a bowl and set aside.
2. Combine cabbage and salt in a large bowl. Set aside until cabbage wilts.
3. In another bowl, place pork mince and oils, and mix well with your hands.
4. Squeeze out water from cabbage and combine with chives, sake, soy sauce, sugar, ginger juice, salt and pepper.
5. Add pork to the cabbage mixture and mix well with your hands.

Dipping Sauce

⅓ cup (80ml/2½ 2fl oz) soy sauce
⅓ cup (80ml/2½ fl oz) rice vinegar
Sesame oil, few drops
Chilli oil, few drops

Dumpling Mixture

100g (3½ oz) Chinese or savoy cabbage, finely chopped
½ teaspoon salt
100g (3½ oz) lean pork mince (ground pork)
1 tablespoon vegetable oil
½ teaspoon sesame oil
10 stems garlic chives, chopped or 1 stem spring onion, trimmed and chopped finely
1 tablespoon sake
½ tablespoon soy sauce
1 teaspoon caster sugar
1 teaspoon ginger juice (made by grating fresh ginger and squeezing over a bowl)
Salt and white pepper, to taste
16 round gyoza or gow gee wrappers
Vegetable oil for frying

6   Holding a gyoza wrapper in the palm of your hand, put about a tablespoonful of filling onto the centre of the wrapper.

7   Dip your index finger in some water and wet in a line around the edge of the wrapper.

8   Fold the wrapper over the filling. Seal the edges together by making small pleats on the top. Repeat with remaining wrappers.

9   Heat some oil on a heated teppan, electric frying pan or barbecue hotplate and place gyoza in rows of 4. Grill one side and turn over with a spatula.

10 Pour ½ cup of water over gyoza, and cover with lid to steam for 1–2 minutes.

11 Serve on a platter or individual plates with dipping sauce.

MAKES 16

Poultry and Eggs

In olden times in Japan, eggs were revered and considered to be messengers from God. In the late Heian Era, eggs were used as offerings and people used to say that if you ate them you would be punished by God. Around the same time, due to the influence of Buddhism and Confucianism introduced from China, the eating of meat was banned. The government issued the law telling people to refrain from the 'destruction of life', and people stopped eating chickens.

In the Azuchimomoyama Era, as the trade between Europeans (Spanish and Portuguese) and the Japanese became prosperous, confectionery such as *castella* (sponge cake) and *bolo* were introduced so people began to use eggs again and because they were so nutritious, eggs became precious.

In the Edo Era (1603–1867), eggs went on sale again and some people started to eat chickens even though the majority still didn't. There are references written at the time introducing the cooking of mainly wild birds such as pheasant, quail, duck, goose, snipe, sparrow, thrush, bulbul and lark. *Yaki-tori* (roast fowl) stands opened up in public. The stall owners made *yakitori* from off-cuts and chunks of chickens from restaurants or other shops and sold them on skewers at open-air stalls on the streets and temple gardens during festival seasons.

The Meiji Restoration in 1879 brought a change in the culture of eating meat for the Japanese people. Around that time chicken dishes were more highly prized than other meat dishes. Eggs were scarce and precious up until the high economic growth of the postwar period and they were used in the diets of sick and weak people as a nutritional supplement. These days, eggs are a very convenient ingredient and are used for *tamago-yaki* (omelette), *cha-wan mushi* (steamed savoury custard) and in many other recipes. In Japan, eggs are eaten raw unlike in most other countries and because of this foreigners may experience a culture shock. Raw eggs can easily cause salmonella food poisoning so we usually only eat raw eggs in limited local areas, which have a background of good hygiene. However, salmonella has been on the increase in recent years and further hygiene management is needed.

What is a 'raw egg' dish? I would say *tamagokake-gohan*, which is raw egg mixed with soy sauce and poured onto hot steaming rice. We also use raw egg for *sukiyaki* (steamboat).

たまごかけご飯

Tamagokake-gohan
Rice Topped with Raw Egg

This is the ultimate in simple egg dishes. However, finding a really fresh egg is the key to this dish because all eggs cannot be eaten raw. I visited a poultry yard in Wakayama where rare traditional Japanese hens are raised free range and lay their slightly larger than usual eggs in the yard. These freshly laid eggs have a smooth texture when eaten, a firm white and a very thick and creamy egg yolk. These are the best eggs to use for Tamago-kake gohan.

1 Break an egg over the rice and eat with soy sauce or soy sauce with dashi.

SERVES 1

1 very fresh egg
1 bowl of cooked rice
Salt-reduced soy sauce
  or soy sauce with bonito dashi

茶碗蒸し

Cha-wan mushi
Steamed Savoury Egg

This delicious dish has a quite runny consistency, unlike many Western 'custard-style' dishes, which are generally firmer.

1 Bring water in a steamer to the boil, then reduce heat to simmer.

2 Meanwhile, prepare egg mixture by combining eggs, dashi, soy and mirin together in a bowl.

3 Strain egg mixture and pour into 2 cups.

4 Add shiitake, chicken and king prawns to egg mixture.

5 Cover each cup with a piece of foil. Carefully place them into the steamer. Steam over low heat for approximately 10 minutes. To check if cooked, insert a skewer into the egg. If ready, clear juice will appear on the surface. Just before serving, top with a mitsuba leaf or snow pea sprouts.

SERVES 2

2 eggs, beaten
1½ cups dashi
1 tablespoon light-coloured
   soy sauce
1 teaspoon mirin
1 small fresh shiitake mushroom
   or 1 dried shiitake mushroom
   soaked in water, sliced
2 cubes of chicken breast fillet
2 small green king prawns,
   peeled and deveined
2 mitsuba or snow pea sprouts

Note
Other ingredients you can add to this dish are one or two fresh asparagus spears, cut into 5cm (2in) lengths, carrot slices or udon noodles. However, since this is a delicate savoury dish, the flavours for the fillings should just filter through the egg custard, not swamp it. Limit the number of fillings to 3 per cup.

石焼親子丼

Ishiyaki Oyako-don
Chicken and Egg on Rice in Hot Bowls

This should be served in individual small stone bowls from Korean shops.

1. Combine ingredients for warishita sauce in a pan and warm up.
2. Add chicken and onion to sauce, then cook for 3–5 minutes.
3. Heat up the stone bowls on the stove.
4. Place rice into each bowl. Remove chicken and onion from warishita sauce and place on rice.
5. Top with 2 eggs per bowl.
6. Pour over warishita sauce and top with mitsuba
7. To serve, carefully place bowls on heat resistant place mats and take care not to burn yourself as the bowls stay extremely hot for a long time.
8. As you eat, mix the egg through all the ingredients.

SERVES 4

Warishita sauce
2 tablespoons soy sauce
1 tablespoon mirin
2 tablespoons caster sugar
1 cup (250ml/8fl oz) bonito dashi

320g chicken breast fillet, sliced into 20g (½ oz) pieces
1 onion, peeled and sliced
8 cups cooked rice
8 eggs
8 mitsuba (Japanese water cress)

チキン南蛮

Nanban-Chiken

Vinaigrette Chicken

1 Soak onion in water for 30 minutes, then drain.
2 In a pan, boil vinegar and sake to evaporate the alcohol. Remove from the heat, add soy sauce, sugar and chilli and stir. Add onion. Set aside as marinade.
3 Mix the sake, mirin, soy sauce, ginger, salt, pepper and sansho in a bowl. Cut chicken into 5cm (2in) pieces and soak in the sauce, massaging with your hands to combine thoroughly.
4 Gradually add potato starch to eggs and whisk together.
5 In a deep frying pan, heat oil over medium heat.
6 Dip the chicken into the batter, then deep fry.
7 Drain the chicken well, then place in the marinade for about 15 minutes.
8 Serve with lemon slices.

SERVES 4

2 small white or brown onions, peeled and thinly sliced
150ml (5fl oz) rice vinegar
250ml (8fl oz) sake
2 tablespoons soy sauce
2 tablespoons caster sugar
1–2 red chillies, de-seeded and sliced
1 tablespoon sake
2 teaspoons mirin
1 tablespoon soy sauce
1 tablespoon grated ginger
Salt, pinch
Pepper, to taste
Sansho (Japanese mountain pepper), to taste
600g (1¼ lb) chicken breast or thigh fillet
1 tablespoon potato starch
2 eggs, beaten
Vegetable oil for deep frying
1 lemon, sliced

だし巻き卵

Dashimaki-tamago

Japanese Omelette with Dashi

1 Crack the eggs into a bowl and add dashi, mirin, salt and soy sauce. Mix with a pair of chopsticks or a fork.

2 Strain into another bowl.

3 Heat up a non-stick frying pan over a medium heat and drop in a little oil and swirl evenly over the pan.

4 Pour in one third of the egg mixture and cook until set around the edges.

5 With a spatula, fold one-third towards the front of the pan, then fold over again in the same direction onto the remaining portion.

6 Add a little more oil to the pan and pour half of the remaining egg mixture onto the empty area of the pan. Tilt the pan and lift the edge of the omelette with a spatula so that the mixture flows under the folded egg. Cook until the edges sets.

7 Again fold one-third towards the folded egg, then fold this over on top of previous roll, making a flat roll on one side of the pan.

8 Add more oil and pour in the remaining egg mixture, and repeat the folding process. Give a little push to mould the shape with the spatula.

9 When cooked, remove from the heat, and place on a bamboo mat on a dry surface. Wrap the omelette with the bamboo mat and place a thick chopstick to make a hole as a decoration. It can also be left as a cylinder or squared off.

10 Cut the omelette into pieces. In the hole, place grated daikon and okra. Serve with soy sauce.

5 medium eggs

⅓ cup dashi (see page 78)

1 tablespoon mirin

⅓ teaspoon salt

Light-coloured soy sauce, few drops

Vegetable oil

2 tablespoon grated daikon-radish

1 okra, trimmed and blanched

Soy sauce, to serve

Nori flakes, to garnish (optional)

SERVES 4

Pancakes, Noodles and Other Teppanyaki Treats

O utside of Japan, teppanyaki is usually understood to be a meal of steak or seafood with vegetables cooked on a teppan hotplate. However, in Japan, two of the most popular *teppanyaki* meals are *okonomiyaki* and *yakisoba* noodles. *Okonomiyaki*, a type of pancake or omelette, originated in the Kansai area near Osaka, so naturally there have been many restaurants in that area specialising in *okonomiyaki* for a long time, but these days they are also found throughout Japan. They are usually very reasonably priced, and provide a tasty, filling meal.

Most Japanese tend to eat *okonomiyaki* at a restaurant or one of the many small food outlets, but in Kansai people commonly cook it at home using an electric hotplate.

お好み焼き

Okonomiyaki Osaka-style

Okonomiyaki Savoury Pancake

1 To make pancake batter, combine dashi powder with water in a large bowl. Add the other batter ingredients and whisk well.

2 In a small bowl, gently fold together ¼ of the cabbage, ¼ of the batter mixture and 1 egg. Do not mix.

3 Make pancakes one by one. On high heat, drop 1 tablespoon of oil on a heated teppan, electric frying pan or barbecue hotplate and pour on the batter mixture.

4 Place 3 pork slices on top of the pancake. When bubbles appear on the surface, lower heat to medium and cook for 3 minutes.

5 Using two spatulas, turn the pancake over and press down firmly with a spatula.

6 Break an egg beside the pancake on the hotplate. Using a corner of the spatula, break the egg yolk. Turn the pancake over onto the egg. Push any leaking egg in towards the pancake to cook, keeping the shape of the pancake neat.

7 When the egg is cooked, turn the pancake over again. Brush with sauce, dollop with mayonnaise and sprinkle with ao-nori.

8 Repeat this process to make three more pancakes.

SERVES 4

Pancake Batter

1 teaspoon katsuo dashi (bonito stock) powder

250ml (8 fl oz) water

200g (7oz) plain flour (weak flour is preferable)

10g (⅓ oz) yamaimo (yam potato) powder or 80g (3oz) frozen yamaimo, grated

1 teaspoon salt

400g (14oz) cabbage, trimmed and chopped

4 eggs

4 tablespoons vegetable oil or lard

12 paper-thin slices pork, approximately 30g (1oz) each

Okonomiyaki sauce (available from Japanese grocers)

Japanese mayonnaise

Ao-nori (dried green seaweed) powder

Note

Another variation of okonomiyaki known as modanyaki (modern-style okonomiyaki), includes the addition of yakisoba noodles (Japanese-style egg noodle). Instead of pork, you can use peeled king prawns, cuttlefish, oysters, cheese, chicken or dried shrimps.

焼きそば

Yakisoba

Yakisoba Stir-fry

1 Cook noodles and drain well.
2 Heat oil in a pan and add garlic, sliced pork, cabbage, carrot, shiitake and spring onion, stirring all the while.
3 Season to taste.
4 Make sauce by combining all ingredients.
5 Add noodles and sauce to pan while still stirring.
6 Place onto individual plates and top with red pickled ginger, green nori or bonito flakes.

SERVES 2

300g (10½ oz) yakisoba noodles
Vegetable oil
1 garlic clove, chopped
100g (4oz) sliced pork fillet
2 cabbage leaves, cut into small pieces
½ carrot, peeled and sliced
2 fresh or dried shiitake mushrooms
1 spring onion, sliced diagonally
Salt and white pepper, to taste

Yakisoba sauce

2 tablespoons tomato sauce
2 tablespoons Worcestershire sauce
1 tablespoon dashi
1 tablespoon soy sauce
1 tablespoon honey

Garnishes

Red pickled ginger
Aonori (green nori flakes) or bonito flakes

Note

Yakisoba is a very versatile dish. You can add almost any vegetable from your fridge, such as mushrooms, onion, capsicum or asparagus as well as seafood or chicken.

Instead of egg noodles, you can use udon noodles.

You can cook yakisoba on the barbecue.

Commercially prepared yakisoba sauce is available from Japanese or Asian groceries.

Tempura

Tempura is eaten everywhere in Japan, in every venue, from *tachigui*, the fast food no-seat-eat stands, to high-class restaurants. Throughout the West it has become quite a familiar food, on equal footing with *sushi* and *sukiyaki* as representative of all Japanese cooking. It is the ultimate in enjoyment; seasonal food covered in a light crispy, non-greasy batter.

The basic tempura batter ingredients, what we call tane or neta, are plain flour, eggs and water. In early times, battered vegetables were called *shojin-age* and tempura referred only to battered seafood. These days, tempura includes both vegetable and seafood varieties.

Typical tempura tane are prawns, squid, eggplant, *shishito* (Japanese green pepper), *satsuma-imo* (sweet potato) and *kabocha* (pumpkin), but a great variety of seafood and vegetables may be used, depending on the season. This seasonal effect is not so obvious in Western countries where tempura fillings are usually fairly predictable. Meat is rarely used as a tempura ingredient. Deep- fried meat is more likely to be coated in breadcrumbs, or simply deep fried with no coating as in kara- age.

Tempura is a simple method of cooking, but the end result depends on the skilful techniques of the chef. The skill lies in creating deep-fried morsels coated in a light, crisp and airy batter, with no sogginess or oiliness, encasing a luscious, moist interior, never overcooked. At specialty tempura bars, in front of the waiting diners on the other side of the counter, the chef dexterously slices the fish and vegetables, dips and deep fries them and serves them to the customers in the same way the *sushi* chefs serve *sushi*. The dynamic techniques have an instant impact on the observers, which stimulates their artistic appreciation as well as their appetites. Not only is it a joy to eat, it is a pleasure to watch.

There is always some debate about the origin of the name tempura and the cooking method itself, but it is generally accepted that this style of deep frying was introduced into the Nagasaki region by the Portuguese in the 17th century, firstly as a vegetable dish, with seafood being introduced later in the Edo period. At that time, Tokyo was expanding rapidly and tempura street stalls became understandably popular as part of the bustling metropolitan lifestyle.

The aroma of deep-frying food wafting through the streets and the novelty of standing at a counter to eat this new style of food would have been a great attraction. With the introduction of luxury ingredients such as eggs and oil, tempura gained a certain status among the upper classes. Its reputation as a quality food has remained ever since.

Occasionally tempura is served with nothing more than a squeeze of citrus juice, but more often it is served with a dipping sauce of one sort or another, depending on the filling. *Tentsuyu* is a common dipping sauce, consisting of soy sauce and stock with the addition of grated *daikon*, either on its own or with chilli or ginger. Sometimes we add salt or green tea salt, curry salt, *yuzu salt* (Japanese citrus) or *sansho* (mountain pepper).

天麩羅

Tempura

1. Mix flour and potato starch in a bowl to make tempura batter. Gradually add refrigerated cold water and gently combine using a pair of chopsticks or a fork.
2. To prepare prawns, remove the head and shell without cutting off the tail, then devein.
3. Heat oil in a deep pan to about 180°C (350°F). To check the temperature, drop a small amount of the tempura batter into the oil, and when it quickly floats up, it is ready.
4. Coat prawns and vegetables with extra potato starch.
5. Holding one ingredient at a time with tongs, chopsticks or your fingers (the last is easier but dangerous) dip it into the batter and then carefully slide it into the oil. Do not put too many ingredients in at one time, ingredients must be able to float freely and too many at once will bring down the temperature of the oil.
6. Drain on paper towel. Sprinkle with salts and garnish with lemon wedges to serve.

SERVES 4

250g tempura flour or 100g flour
   and 50g potato starch
250ml cold water
8 prawns (shrimp)
4 slices sweet potato
   or pumpkin, chopped
4 asparagus or French beans,
   sliced
8 slices lotus root
Vegetable oil for deep frying
Extra potato starch for coating
Salt
Mattcha salt
Curry salt
Lemon wedges

天丼
Tendon
Tempura on Rice

1. Prepare tempura.
2. Combine all the ingredients for sauce in a saucepan and bring to the boil over a high heat. Simmer over low heat for 3 minutes.
3. Place warm rice in each bowl, top with tempura, then pour over the sauce.

SERVES 2

6 tempura king prawns
  or tempura of your choice
  (see page 200)

Sauce
⅔ cup dashi
1 tablespoon soy sauce
1 tablespoon mirin
1 teaspoon caster sugar

2 bowls cooked rice, warmed

Sweets for My Sweet

Kashi is Japanese for sweet foods—desserts, lollies, or biscuits—but actually derives from the word for fruit. It also covers such snacks as chips and rice crackers. With a prefix it is written and pronounced ...*gashi*, as in *wagashi* —sweets made by traditional Japanese methods. We take sweets for granted these days, but there was a time when *wagashi* were only sent to the Imperial Palace, legal courts, temples or tea houses, either as a gift, a form of homage or as a regular agreement between those establishments and a *wagashi* provider.

Traditional Japanese desserts were not rich, often just fruit—persimmons, particularly dried persimmons, grapes, nashi pears and mandarins. Now there are many introduced fruits, but good quality fruit can be quite expensive. In many households the mother cuts pieces of fruit and shares them out to the family after meals. In winter, my mother bought mandarins from a farmer. I loved to eat them sitting at the *kotatsu* (low Japanese table with a heat source beneath it).

Historically, Japanese sweets have always been influenced by overseas trade. Long ago, *togashi* (Chinese sweets) were introduced from China and Korea. In the Kamakura Era, Buddhist monks brought in *tenshin* (Chinese-style morning tea), which includes some *togashi* such as a small cake with a walnut centre. In the late 16th century, many sweets were introduced from Europe by the Portuguese and referred to as *nanbangashi* or *yogashi*. Two popular examples still eaten today are *kastera* (Madeira cake) and *karameru* (caramel).

From the 17th century onwards, sweets not only tasted good, but presentation became a driving force. The true essence of Japanese artistry came to the fore. The tea ceremony is a spiritual, ritualistic event, so artistic presentation of the sweets became very important.

Themes developed depicting the essence of each season. For instance, *kuzu* (arrowroot starch) is used for translucent sweets, suggesting the cooling effect of a block of ice. Other ingredients reflect natural elements such as the birds and flowers of spring or autumn leaves, the wind and the moon. Some sweets are so beautiful that it seems almost a pity to eat them; you feel like putting them in your pocket and taking them home.

Wagashi may be eaten with *usucha* (light green tea) or *koicha* (strong green tea), not necessarily in the formal tea ceremony. The sweetness of *wagashi* contrasts with the bitterness of the green tea. More often than not, *usucha* is accompanied by *higashi* (dried sweets), but also *senbei*, (savoury biscuits). *Higashi* are compressed, moulded sweets, often powdery and dry in texture, in the shape of pink or white flowers. Other sweets, called *namagashi*, have a higher moisture content of around 40 per cent, come in a variety of shapes, colours and textures and are eaten with strong green tea. *Yokan* (firm red bean paste) and *monaka* (thin wafers with red bean paste filling) are two examples of *namagashi*.

Most *yogashi* (Western-style desserts) are available in Japan and are usually served after a meal. They are also served with afternoon tea and many cafes specialise in this fashion. True Japanese desserts usually consist simply of beautifully presented fruit, but Japanese chefs are now creating 'cross-over' desserts—an enjoyable blend of both styles, with a typical Japanese twist.

On the outskirts of Kyoto, only three stops from Kyoto Central, there is a small *kashi* business currently run by Mr Kitagawa, master of *wagashi* and before him, by his father, who was master of *mamegashi* (bean desserts) and his father before him. Having been so deeply entrenched in the *wagashi* family business, Mr Kitagawa decided to study Western-style sweets in Tokyo to develop a good overview of both techniques. He has become so popular in the local district that he only wishes to concentrate all his efforts locally and maintain his reputation as one of the finest *wagashi* makers rather than expanding into other districts or products. One of his specialities is a glutenous *manjuu* wrapped in bamboo leaves which is quite famous in the area of Nagaokakyu where he works. He is a stickler for detail, supervising every step scrupulously. A total purist, he uses mineral water from a spring in his garden when making *warabi-mochi*. *Warabi* powder is readily available from supermarkets, but he insists on using a particular powder from a local producer and a secret recipe passed down through the family. There is apparently something in the technique of leaving the mixture to stand overnight which, as it cools down, produces a more starchy texture and a richer flavour, the unique features of his *warabi-mochi*. He adds a signature touch by coating them with a powder called *kinako* made from soybean bran.

どら焼き (ズンダ｡つぶあん)

Dora-yaki (zunda and tubuan)
Japanese Pancake with Green Soy Beans
and Red Bean Jam

1   To make the zunda jam, cook eda-mame for 7–8
    minutes if fresh; as per directions on the package for
    frozen; and drain. Remove the hull. Using a mortar and
    a pestle or food processor, grind, then add sugar and
    salt and mix well.
2   To make pancakes, sift the flour, then whisk in the egg
    and sugar.
3   Mix honey and baking powder together with a spatula.
    Then add to flour and combine well.
4   Gradually add water into the pancake mixture and
    mix well.
5   Cover with plastic wrap and set aside for 30 minutes.
6   Heat oil in a frying pan and make small pancakes of
    approximately 10cm (4ins) across.
7   Sandwich together with jam.

MAKES 8

Jam
100g (3oz) fresh or frozen
    eda-mame (green soy beans)
70g (2½ oz) caster sugar
Salt, pinch

Pancake
80g (3oz) plain four
1 egg
70g (2½ oz) sugar
1 tablespoon honey
⅓ tablespoon baking soda,
    mixed with a teaspoon water
40ml (1½ fl oz) water
Vegetable oil
80g (3oz) sweet tsubu-an
    (red bean paste

Note
Eda-mame is available from Japanese grocery shops. Zunda is
another term for the more familiar dish using eda-mame and
is popular in sweets in the Tohoku region (North East Japan),
particularly in Sendai.

Fruit

If asked about the typical Japanese fruits I would answer 'persimmon and citrus', which have a long history dating back to their arrival from China many centuries ago and, of course, the nashi pear. Sweetness in fruit is important in Japan where it plays an important role as dessert.

Persimmons have a lot of Vitamin C; dried persimmons keep well, are sweeter and retain their vitamins, so were a very useful fruit in the past.

Japanese citrus such as *natsu-mikan*, harvested in summer, and mandarin in winter are used fresh or in preserves. Cumquat is another popular citrus and a popular dessert when reduced with sugar to a thick sauce. Citrus fruits such as *yuzu*, *sudachi* and *kabosu* provide a dash of accent in cooking. In winter, some people add *yuzu* to a bath for the aroma and for relaxation.

Nashi pears come in two types, red- and green-skinned. Compared to Western pears, *nashi* are crunchier and have a more refined sweetness, in my opinion. *Choujyuurou* (a red-skinned *nashi*) was found in the private garden of Touma Choujuurou around the Meiji Era (1867–1912). It looks like a large, round apple. The other popular red-skinned varieties are *kousui* and *toyomizu*. The masterpiece of the green-skinned *nashi* family is the *nijusseiki*. It was discovered by chance in Chiba-ken at the turn of the 20th century. *Niju* means twenty and *sseiki* means century. Its paler skin and improved taste has led to it being successfully sold overseas.

During the 20th century, many varieties of fruit were introduced from America and Europe, including apples, strawberries and cherries. Japanese farmers set about breeding fruit to suit local tastes. They produced original Japanese fruit that are now popular at home and overseas. For example, *Fuji* apples, a large, less acidic and sweeter apple and sweet, soft *Toyonoka* strawberries are exported to the rest of the world.

A popular new variety of pear—La Fracne—was introduced into Japan from France in 1903. They aren't even being produced in Europe any more as the climate there doesn't suit them.

I guess Japanese fruit will continue to evolve in the future.

わらびもち

Warabi-Mochi

Warabi-Mochi Cake

Warabi-mochi is a traditional summer dessert. Originally it was made of wild bracken starch; however, these days it is made of the starch from sweet potatoes and tapioca.

1 Mix warabi-mochi powder with water in a pan, according to the packet instructions.

2 Cook over a low heat until transparent, mixing continuously with a wooden spatula.

3 Moisten a mould or other container with a little water and pour in warabi-mochi.

4 Stand in a bowl of icy water to cool it down.

5 Do not refrigerate or its colour will change to white.

6 While it is cooling down, make the coating.

7 When it's cool, take out and cut into pieces (the size you prefer).

8 Coat with kinako or mattcha-kinako mixture to serve.

SERVES 4

150g packet warabi-mochi powder
Water

Kinako coating

Mix 20g kinako (soybean powder) and 20g caster sugar or jyohakutou (Japanese style of sugar). This is basic. If you like spice, add cinnamon.

Mattcha–kinako coating

Mix 1 teaspoon mattcha (green tea powder), 20g sugar and 15g kinako.

Note
Warabi-mochi powder is available from Japanese grocery shops. Jyohakutou is the most common style of sugar in Japan.

白熊アイス

Shirokuma-ice

White Bear Shaved Ice

Shaved ice reminds me of summer—the taste is sweet and refreshing in the heat and children love it. Traditionally it is flavoured with coloured syrups, condensed milk or sweet red beans but modern versions may include chocolate or coffee. I found a unique type of shaved ice in Kagoshima, Kyushu, called shirokuma-ice or white bear shaved ice. To make it yourself, you need to make something that looks like a bear face on top of the ice, using fruits or beans. Using coffee will change the white bear into a brown bear, but I think the white bear sounds cool, don't you?

1 Using an ice shaver, shave ice into a glass bowl until densely packed.

2 Push down on the top of the ice with a spoon to make it firm and pour on some condensed milk.

3 Shave more ice over the top.

4 Then pour remaining condensed milk over and decorate with fruit, using raisins to make the eyes and nose of the bear.

5 Top with sweet red bean paste and a cherry.

SERVES 1

ice

condensed milk

1 slice of watermelon

2 slices of kiwi fruit

1 slice of pineapple

1 segment of orange

1 slice of banana

3 large raisins

1 tablespoon tsubuan (pre-made sweet red bean paste)

1 cherry

Cherry Flower Ice-Cream

Green Tea Ice-Cream

Black Sesame Ice-Cream

桜のアイスクリーム

Sakura no aisu kuriimu

Cherry Flower Ice-Cream

1 Whiz sakura flower, cream and milk in a blender,
   then bring to boil in a saucepan. Remove from heat.
2 In a bowl, whisk sugar and egg yolks together until pale.
3 Gradually pour the hot milk mixture into the bowl,
   stirring with a wooden spoon.
4 Make the mixture into custard by cooking over a double
   boiler to the ribbon stage, stirring continuously with
   a wooden spoon.
5 While still hot, strain the mixture into a bowl.
6 Place the bowl in an ice bath until cold and then churn
   mixture in an ice-cream machine.

MAKES 4–6 SCOOPS

10 preserved sakura
   flower petals
150ml (5fl oz) cream
200ml (8fl oz) milk
2 tablespoons caster sugar
3 egg yolks
4 sakura flower petals
   for garnish

抹茶アイスクリーム

Mattcha aisu kuriimu

Green Tea Ice-Cream

1 Make custard following the recipe for cherry flower ice-cream.
2 After the straining stage, add green tea mixture and stir well.
3 Cool in an ice bath until cold and churn in an ice-cream machine.

MAKES 4–6 SCOOPS

150ml (5fl oz) cream
200ml (6fl oz) milk
3 egg yolks
¼ cup caster sugar
¼ cup green tea powder mixed
  with 1 teaspoon water

黒胡麻アイスクリーム

Kurogama aisu kuriimu

Black Sesame Ice-Cream

1 Make custard following the recipe for cherry flower ice-cream.
2 After the straining stage, mix in black sesame seeds.
3 Cool in an ice bath until cold and churn in an ice-cream machine.

MAKES 4–6 SCOOPS

150ml (5fl oz) cream
200ml (6fl oz) milk
3 egg yolks
¼ cup (60ml/2fl oz) caster sugar
2 tablespoons black sesame
  seeds, lightly roasted
  and ground

Beverages

Tea and Japanese food culture have been closely related to each other for a very long time. Cha-Kaiseki-ryouri, a style of meal developed to accompany the tea ceremony, is one of the origins of Japanese cuisine and has had a huge influence on our food culture. These days, people tend to drink more coffee and black tea, but drinking green tea at meals is still part of Japanese life.

I visited Asami-en, a producer of sayama tea, in Sayama city, a sub-centre metropolis near Tokyo where the tea farms are interspersed among residential areas. The picking season is between April and August and when I visited in September it was already over and the tea trees were beautifully pruned. Asami-en has an authentic tearoom where Mrs Asami, dressed in a kimono, served us several kinds of tea from their farm. I enjoyed them immensely as they were flavoursome and sweet.

Green Tea

Japanese green tea is dried without fermentation. After picking the leaves, they are sterilised with steam or roasted. There are various varieties of green teas but *sen-cha* is the most popular and familiar. The best quality of *sen-cha* is called *gyokuro*, which is made only from young leaves covered and protected from the sun for twenty days which means it has less bitterness and a fuller flavour.

To serve sen-cha for 1

1   Choose a small teapot.
2   Pour boiled water into a tea cup. Transfer the water to the pot.
3   Pour the water back into the tea cup.
4   Put approximately 2 teaspoons of green tea leaves into the pot and pour over water from the tea cup.
5   Wait for one minute and serve.

When you make tea in a large teapot, use water between 70–80°C. This is the best temperature to brew the tea.

Genmai-cha is sen-cha green tea combined with roasted unpolished brown rice. It has an aromatic flavour and is quite a refreshing drink. The best temperature to brew it is about 95°C.

Hōi-cha is roasted green tea, which has less caffeine and less bitterness. You can use up stale green tea by roasting the leaves on baking paper in a frying pan over a low heat to make hoji-cha. The best temperature to brew it is about 95°C.

Maccha is powdered green tea. To brew, pour hot water into a tea bowl to warm. Using a *chasen* (bamboo whisk), moisten the bowl then discard the water. Wrap the bowl in a muslin cloth and using a *chashaku* (bamboo teaspoon), add about 2 grams of tea powder and pour about ¼ of a cup of hot water. Whisk with the *chasen*.

Green tea is very delicate; it easily loses quality by exposure to moisture, light and temperature extremes. So it is better to keep it in an airtight box and away from the direct light.

Shōchú

Shōchú is a distilled liquor, unlike sake which is brewed, that can be made from one of several raw ingredients such as rice, sweet potatoes, soba wheat, barley or black sugar. Each version tastes strongly of its source ingredient but its flavour is often described as nutty or earthy and the alcoholic content is usually about 25 per cent. Shōchú is drunk throughout a meal in many forms according to the season or personal taste. This is one of the reasons it is so popular in Japan.

Shōchú can be drunk

- straight
- rokku, on the rocks
- mizu-wari, diluted with water
- oyu-wari, diluted with hot water
- mixed with oolong tea or fruit juice
- chúhai, with tonic water, ice and some flavouring, often lemon, grapefruit, apple or ume (pickled plum).
- mixed with a low-alcohol beer-flavoured beverage known as hoppy.

Shōchú production in Japan is mainly in Kyúshú, Okinawa and the surrounding islands. I visited prestigious shōchú makers Satsuma-Shiramami in Makurazaki, Kagoshima. Kagoshima produces several types of sweet potatoes that are used as the main ingredient of imo-shōchú (sweet potato shōchú).

Koganesengan sweet potatoes make excellent imo-shōchú. They contain high levels of starch and have yellowish white skin with light yellow flesh which makes the shōchú full-bodied and with a deep aroma. Benihayato has light reddish skin with orange flesh. It contains a high level of carotene similar to carrots. Shōchú made from benihayato has an invigorating aroma and elegant texture. Benisatuma has light yellowish flesh. It is good for making sweets.

They have a unique way to drink shōchú in Kagoshima. Combine shōchú and water at a ratio of 6:4 in a special bottle called a kuro-dyokka the day before drinking. The shōchú and water melt together and the flavour becomes rich and mellow. Then warm up it up to enrich the aroma and drink.

The level of dilution and accompanying mixer is a matter of personal taste. This is one of the real charms of drinking shōchú.

Sake

Sake is the most famous Japanese alcohol. The word *sake* has two meanings, one is alcohol in general. The other is a particular drink, *nihon-shu*, which is what I refer to here.

Sake is a fermented beverage, made primarily from rice. It's brewed using a micro-organism called *koji*, with an alcohol content between 13–16 per cent. Brewers take advantage of the various mineral waters in Japan to make excellent sake. There are many varieties of sake, which can be enjoyed warm or chilled, depending on the season.

Like wine, sake varies widely depending on the brewers' skill at handling ingredients and individual techniques. There are three categories I would like to introduce to you called *honjyozo-shu* and *junmai-shu* and *ginjyo-shu*.

Honjyozo-shu

This is made with rice that has been polished until 70 per cent or less of the grain remains, along with *koji-malt*, brewing alcohol and water. The milling removes protein and oils from the exterior of the rice, leaving starch, which creates a harsher environment for yeast. As a result the yeast generates amino acids, citric acid, malic acid and other alkanoic acids to produce flavours and add fruity aromas. *Honjyozoshu* is known for its mild, unobtrusive bouquet and crisp flavour.

Junmai-shu

This is refined or pure sake, containing no additives or distilled alcohol. It has a rich, smooth flavour and purified colour, with a significant texture created by each individual brewer.

Ginjyo-shu

This is made using white rice milled so that 40 per cent or less of the grain remains and may contain brewing alcohol. A fruity, somewhat floral bouquet and a clear, crisp flavour characterise it.

All other types of sake fall under the category of *futsushu*, which is consumed widely throughout Japan. This category offers various tastes, with each brand featuring a unique flavour that is characteristic of the brewery.

Sake is served in a special ceramic or porcelain bottle called a *tokkuri* and drunk from *o-choko*, small individual cups made of ceramic, pottery or glass.

Japanese Beer

Beer is not like *seishu* (refined sake), which has been in Japanese culture for a long time. In the beginning, when beer was first introduced into Japan, it was not popular. People thought it was bitter and without flavour. But in the 1960s, beer left sake behind in terms of consumption in Japan and the market has been continuously growing and people drink beer all year round. Nowadays, drinking beer is one of the things that reminds people of summer. Beer gardens have sprung up and especially in summer attract people to come together to drink chilled beer accompanied with *edamame* (boiled fresh green soy beans) or cold tofu. I have also frequently seen people toasting with beer when dining. Beer is now one of the necessities of Japanese life and has the privilege of being included in the food culture of Japan.

In the Edo Era (1603–1867), the Dutch introduced beer into Japan. At this time only the people who wanted contact with Western culture tried to drink beer. In the Meiji Era, Mr William Copeland (1832–1902), a Norwegian-born American made the first beer in Japan. He came to Yokohama at the age of 35, having learnt brewing techniques for five years from a German engineer. He found a spring water pond called Tennuma in Yokohama. He made beer with the water to test the quality, which was successful. He then built a brewery and called it Spring Valley Brewery. This was the dawn of beer history in Japan. Today, the Kirin Beer Company is located on this site. Japanese beer companies had to overcome difficult times to attain success. Nowadays, there are many brands such as Kirin, Sapporo, Asahi and Ebisu. They compete with each other to create beers suitable for Japanese taste.

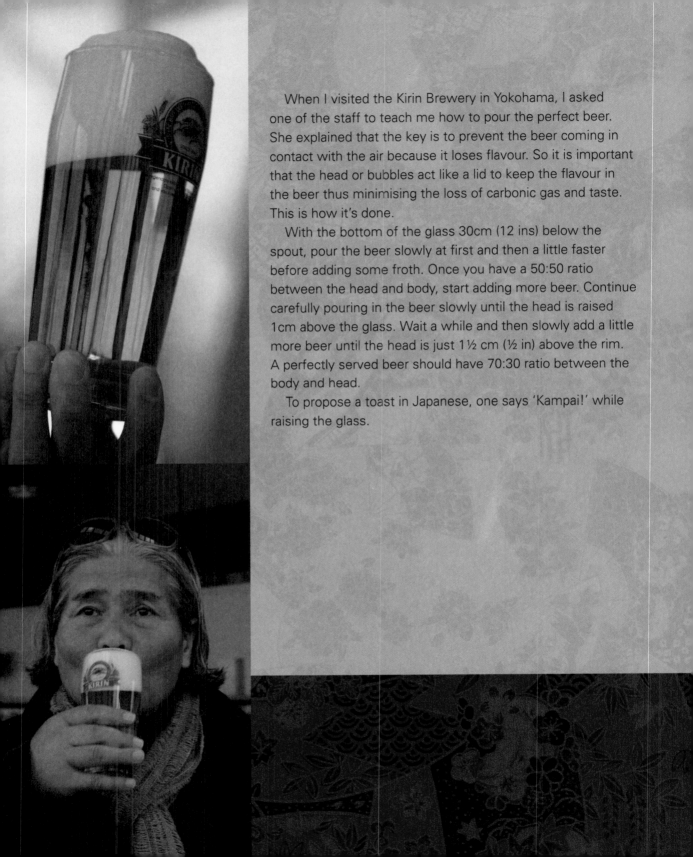

When I visited the Kirin Brewery in Yokohama, I asked one of the staff to teach me how to pour the perfect beer. She explained that the key is to prevent the beer coming in contact with the air because it loses flavour. So it is important that the head or bubbles act like a lid to keep the flavour in the beer thus minimising the loss of carbonic gas and taste. This is how it's done.

With the bottom of the glass 30cm (12 ins) below the spout, pour the beer slowly at first and then a little faster before adding some froth. Once you have a 50:50 ratio between the head and body, start adding more beer. Continue carefully pouring in the beer slowly until the head is raised 1cm above the glass. Wait a while and then slowly add a little more beer until the head is just 1½ cm (½ in) above the rim. A perfectly served beer should have 70:30 ratio between the body and head.

To propose a toast in Japanese, one says 'Kampai!' while raising the glass.

Recipe List

Index